THE MIDNIGHT

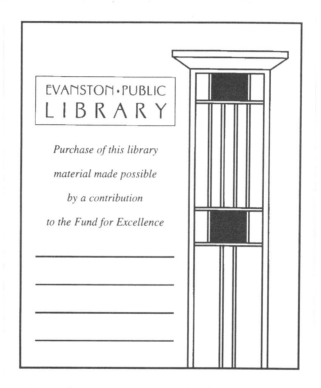

THE MIDNIGHT

SUSAN HOWE

A NEW DIRECTIONS BOOK

Grateful acknowledgments: The photograph of the double map illustration by William Hole from *Poly-Olbion* by Michael Drayton is reproduced by permission of the Beinecke Rare Book and Manuscript Library, Yale University. The photograph of the Emily Dickinson manuscript 169 is reproduced by permission of the Trustees of Amherst College and the President and Fellows of Harvard College. The photograph of the Charles Sanders Peirce manuscript 495 (1898) is reproduced by permission of the Houghton Library, Harvard University. The photograph of the portrait of an unknown man formerly known as Michael Drayton, by an unknown artist, is reproduced courtesy of the National Portrait Gallery, London. The photograph of Cornelius Janssen's 1617 portrait of Mary Ferrar is reproduced courtesy of the Master and Fellows, Magdalene College, Cambridge, England. Excerpt from T. S. Eliot's "Little Gidding," in *Four Quartets,* copyright 1942 by T. S. Eliot and renewed by Esme Valerie Eliot, reprinted by permission of Harcourt, Inc., in the United States, and, in Canada, from *Collected Poems 1909–1962* by T. S. Eliot, reprinted by permission of Faber & Faber, Ltd., London, England.

Author's Note: I wish to thank Peter Hare for advice and criticism during the composition of "Scare Quotes I and II." The door to the reading room at Harvard University's Houghton Library has been changed since 1991: it now has glass panes and in that regard is more user-friendly.

Publisher's Note: Portions of *The Midnight* have originally appeared in the following books, chapbooks and magazines: Portions of "Bed Hangings I" and "Scare Quotes I" were published in *Bed Hangings* with illustrations by Susan Bee (Granary Books, New York, 2001); portions of "Scare Quotes I and II" and "Kidnapped" were published in *Conjunctions* (2001); portions of "Scare Quotes" appeared in an essay titled "Either ether," published in *Close Listening,* ed. Charles Bernstein (Oxford University Press, 2000); portions of "Bed Hangings II" were published in *Hambone* (2002), *Van Gogh's Ear* (2002), *Literary Imagination* (2003), *Daedalus* (2003), and *American Women Poets in the 21st Century* (ed. Claudia Rankine and Juliana Spahr, Wesleyan University Press, 2002).

Photographs by Peter Hare, edited by Susan Howe
Manufactured in the United States of America
New Directions Books are printed on acid-free paper.
First published as New Directions Paperbook 956 in 2003
Published simultaneously in Canada by Penguin Canada Books, Ltd.

LIBRARY OF CONGRESS CATALOGING-IN-PUBLICATION DATA
Howe, Susan, 1937–
The midnight / Susan Howe.
p. cm. -- (New Directions paperbook ; 956)
ISBN 0-8112-1538-5 (alk. paper)
I. Title.
PS3558.O893 M.
811'.54—dc21

2003003870

New Directions Books are published for James Laughlin
by New Directions Publishing Corporation
80 Eighth Avenue, New York 10011

THE MIDNIGHT

Contents

THE
MASTER OF BALLANTRAE

A Winter's Tale

BY

ROBERT LOUIS STEVENSON

Author of "Kidnapped," "Treasure Island"
&c. &c. &c.

WITH TEN FULL-PAGE ILLUSTRATIONS BY W. HOLE R.S.A.

TWENTY-FOURTH THOUSAND

CASSELL AND COMPANY, LIMITED
LONDON, PARIS & MELBOURNE

ALL RIGHTS RESERVED

MASTER OF BALLANTRAE

There was a time when bookbinders placed a tissue interleaf between frontispiece and title page in order to prevent illustration and text from rubbing together. Although a sign is understood to be consubstantial with the thing or being it represents, word and picture are essentially rivals. The transitional space between image and scripture is often a zone of contention. Here we must separate. Even printers and binders drift apart. Tissue paper for wrapping or folding can also be used for tracing. Mist-like transience. Listen, quick rustling. If a piece of sentence left unfinished can act as witness to a question proposed by a suspected ending, the other side is what will happen. Stage snow. Pantomime.

"Give me a sheet.

The counterfeit presentment of two papers. After 1914, advances in printing technology rendered an interleaf obsolete. Mischief delights in playing with surfaces. Today each spectral scrap intact in a handed down book has acquired an enchanted aura quite apart from its original utilitarian function. Wonderfully life-like, approaching transparency, not shining; this pale or wanly yellow, tangible intangible murderously gentle exile, mutely begs to be excused. Superstition remains—as spiritual hyphen. Listen, quick rustling. In second character, freed from practical obligation, I'm not asleep just leafing. Miniature scenery. Etiquette.

On your side, with pleasure."

BED HANGINGS I

Lady M.
    O proper stuff!
        —*Macbeth*; III. iv

Eugénie. The exertions of the sisters have been most successful. In 1842 they received the gold medal for

Fig. 99.

AVE MARIA.—Dieppe.

having, by the substitution of the Valenciennes for the old Dieppe stitch, introduced a new industry into the depart-

For here we are here

B E D H A N G I N G S

daylight does not reach

Vast depth on the wall

Neophyte

Alapeen Paper Patch Muslin

Calico Camlet Dimity Fustian

Serge linsey-woolsey say

A wainscot bedsted & Curtans

& vallains & iron Rodds

Many bedsteds were roped

"Bedsted. . . . & bed Rope

Revisionist work in

historic interiors spread

from House to Museum

Other documentary evidence

Friends who wish to

remain anonymous

Contest between two

singers *Conflictus ovis*

et lini if the heart or

eye were cause of sin

Rival claims Summer

Winter Soul Body Wine

Water Phillis Flora

Ordered wigs cloaks

breeches hoods gowns

rings jewels necklaces

to be brought together

One of the perplexing questions

on which members of the Bed

Curtain Seminar were able to

shed very little light was that of

how early valences attached

to the tester frame **Technical Note**

Other rubbish a bottomless chair

Go too—my savage pattern

on surface material the line

in ink if you have curtains

and a New English Dictionary

there is nothing to justify a

claim for linen except a late

quotation knap warp is flax

Fathom we without cannot

Research project the 1960

Bed Hangings Symposium

Scholar student participant

Published papers remain

Say flowing forces haunt

leaving no shade pattern

Why huntress why pattern

A small swatch bluish-green

woolen slight grain in the

weft watered and figured

right fustian should hold

altogether warp and woof

Is the cloven rock misled

Does morning lie what prize

What pine tree wildeyed boy

Nor hemp to pleasure pillow

Nor clay scorn to cover as if

sphere of the pent lake hold

Infold me bird and briar you

fathom we cannot to another

declare character in written

summit granite cramp marble

Simple except a blank that it

Present present *presentness*

High mahogany bed roods &

raills do ring loop ties back

A sets down and C takes up

conformity to that uniformity

Ownership and ownership it

is a maxim of logic the Double

of the object is that I desire it

Glide my shadow through

time curtains will dwindle

Far be it from me whatever

reaction splits into willing

things absolute but absent

are not alone Nominalism

While I lie in you for refuge

it is sanctuary it is refuge

Three friends who wish to

remain anonymous a first

design how it was nursed

for cimmerian subtlety for

versification a counterpane

has no reason being agent

Whilst for an absent friend—

Low adamantine net fringe

Surviving fragment of

New England original

bed hanging handsome

cambleteen red curtain

(1746) "a sort of fine

worsted cambels" Camlet

Imitation camlet scrap

To describe Camlet I will

look into Chambers and

Postlethwayt

1746 (fig. 39) A figured
head cloth worked by
Polly Wright of Hatfield
Massachusetts in 1765
(privately owned) This
curtain fabric of "moreen"
by a donor born in 1836
A swatch and swatches
described as "harateen"
Owner John Holker 1850

Counterforce bring me wild hope

non-connection is itself distinct

connection numerous surviving

fair trees wrought with a needle

the merest decorative suggestion

in what appears to be sheer white

muslin a tree fair hunted Daphne

Thinking is willing you are wild

to the weave not to material itself

Upon the interpreter this ambush

Theory at war with phenomena

Thought or form handsbreadth

though paper tossed overboard

can have been conversely tossed

back to background as if woof

warp theory the real what is real

Night draws the planet tremulous

Tinsel hope I intersect linen silk

The ego securely undaunted elect

as pedigree might seem to sound

Example reveals pierced interval

eyelet holes though admittedly if

emblem tossed it lends progress

a corporeal incorporeal European

argument of intellectual sympathy

Sphere of the pent lake hold flint

The ambush lay in wanton purpose

To the Compiler of Memories

Frequent exposure to night air
An inattention to the necessity
of changing damp clothes

Sweet affliction sweet affliction
Singing as I wade to heaven

Soon swerved from what

people of his charge took him

to be

Not only alone but on foot

with his luggage on his back

On the first of January 1801

Something over against is

what surprised the sadder

and wiser

Sandemanian sentiments of
course he never preached as
the denomination admits no
correlative save Christ and his
apostles for the rote of ethic
Embracing the sentiments of
the Sandemanians he was dis-
missed and his apostle until
the church became extinct a
study of odd relic aforesaid

I am going to confine myself

beneath disguises a catalogue

of categories relative to coevel

apostle represented as a plain

if practical preacher I come to

you with neither crook nor shoe

nor scrip a Presbyterian cloak

though admittedly eyelet holes

As if two weathercocks refer

to another class of settlement

You disconcert a maxim
of Pragmatism scorning
small doses of induction
Pragmaticism so far as it
goes if A is true C is true
What is it that is absolute
This is not shown at all
Proceeding to the wood
along with some coeval
you hope to fell a first tree

You are he who felled by

tree deducts the maxims

of Pragmaticism scorning

by a point propitious ab-

duction hedged by paper

you appear to me walking

across the text to call an

unconverted soul King James

lyricism another C minor

Coeval decades hereafter

Ten thousandth truth

Ten thousandth impulse

Do not mince matter

as if tumbling were apt

parable preached in

hedge-sparrow gospel

For the lily welcomes

Owl! art thou mad?

Why dost thou twit me

with foreknowledge

To this the Nihtegale

gave answer that twig

of thine thou shouldst

sing another tune Owl

Still in Ovid cloth of

scarlet the Owl and her

"Old Side" blue thread

Listen! Let me speak!

the Wren replied I do

not want lawlessness

Everyone knows in a rough way

the impious history of sensation

Earlier times resemble ice to the

fourth parish or enthusiast class

Sheets and pillows are initiated

Permanent thought permanent

Before inviolate love knots are

edged with paper in the manner

of braided binding valences before

a long night's sleep with closure

Subject to experience Mr. Sprout

was sent as a vagrant person

from constable to constable

Sandemanian views have not

spread though they have not

become extinct as rapidly as

might be expected in Andrew

Fuller's *Works* whether this

is true or not is a question of

experience in itself sensation

Evening for the Owl

spoke wisely and well

willing to suffer them

and come flying night

from the Carolingian

mid owl falcon fable

In their company saw

all things clearly wel

Unfele I could not do

Nihtegale to the taunt

Owl a preost be piping

Overgo al spoke iseon

sede warme inome nv

stille one bare worde

Go he started mid ivi

Grene al never ne nede

Song long ago al so

sumere chorless awey

Milk they drink and also whey they
know not otherwise bitter accent
I do not remember any crying out
falling down or fainting to signify
revelation preached from Isaiah 60
I have not known visions trances
Who are they that fly as a cloud as
doves to their windows have pity
From terrible and deep conviction
Brandish unreconciled yet arrows

Pensive itinerants and exhorters

gathering manna in the morning

Thirty pages then the rest mostly

children enact ruin enthusiastical

impressions in my mind though

not to my knowledge it seems he

still believed he was conversing

with an invisible spirit however

the sharp weather his wet jacket

Finding himself alive went home

On Our Most Beautiful and Precious Beaker

In 1668 another beaker thought

necessary for the large Meeting

House built in 1713 was the gift of

Madame Ruth Naughty who had

given her black slave Moses to Mr.

Fowler she bequeathed £4 to

purchase the beaker which bears

her name

Something Over Against Mr. Sprout

He can be found in the cool

of evening rolling in his

chaise with his shepherdess

Wearing a large Presbyterian

cloak somewhat soiled with

a full bestowed wig a month

or six weeks diligence will

teach him the exercise of

the windpipe

Some prepared cloth or other

left simply in the hair "glazed"

or "lustred" a kind of twilled

lasting when stouter John Legg

of Boston left to his daughter

1 Coach bed camblet curtanot

vallens to disenchant blessing

All lands and to the bordering

Malachy Postlethwayt (ed. 1773)
defines Calamanco as "a woolen
stuff manufactured in Brabant
in Flanders" checquered in warp
wherein the warp is mixed with
silk or with goat's hair diversely
wrought yet some are quite plain
When did appearance ever justify

It is requested that those who

discover errors in this work

not mentioned in the ERRATA

should give information of them

to Mr. William L. Kingsley of

New Haven and if it seems

desirable they will be given to

the public together with other

facts and statistics ADDENDA

The great Disposer of events

is exchanging what was good

for what is better history that

is written will be accomplished

Stille one bare worde

iseon at bare beode

iseon at bare beode

Fleao westerness iseo

Opertuo go andsware

SCARE QUOTES I

Macb.
      —Now o'er the one half-world
Nature seems dead, and wicked dreams abuse
The curtain'd sleep:
         —*Macbeth*; II. 1.

Some mother loves her child.

Every mother loves her child.

Something loves every child of which it is mother.

I am an insomniac who goes to bed in a closet.

"AWAKE, *a.* Not sleeping; in a state of vigilance or action." "AWAKENING, *n.* A revival of religion, or more general attention to religion than usual." Although these are Noah Webster's definitions, out of his writing speaks Calvin. For Calvin the Bible contains two kinds of knowledge—ecstatic union and law. In *An American Dictionary of the English Language* a curtain is a cloth hanging used in theaters to conceal the stage from the spectators, while an itinerant is someone who travels from place to place and is unsettled; particularly a preacher. One Sunday afternoon in the gift shop at Hartford's Wadsworth Athenaeum, wandering among the postcards, notepaper, ties, scarves, necklaces, key chains, calendars, magic markers, pens, pencils, posters, children's games, paperweights, and art books, displayed to be worshipped or acquired, my attention came to rest on a pedestrian gray paperback. I was preparing to teach a graduate seminar on what has been called "The Great Awakening" of the 1740s. This intercolonial religious revival, with its growth of an itinerant ministry and field sermons, swept through the Connecticut River Valley, then considered back country, in the wake of the arrival of the English evangelist George Whitefield in 1739 (David Garrick said Whitefield could make his hearers weep or tremble at pleasure, by his varied utterance of the word "Mesopotamia") and Jonathan Edwards' restrained but furious eloquence ("Sinners in the Hands of an Angry God; A Sermon Preached at Enfield, July 8th 1741. At a Time of Great Awakenings; and attended with remarkable Impressions on many of the Hearers"). When Europe enters the space of its margin, the "Kingdom of God in America" receives European memory into itself. In thin places bedsteads confront their own edges. English actors and English ministers play key roles in eighteenth century Revivalism. Sometimes charismatic itinerant ministers have no doctrinal or institutional affiliations. Field beds have canopies at the top resembling tents. *Bed Hangings: A Treatise on Fabrics and Styles in the Curtaining of Beds, 1650–1850* with its drab cover illustration, a detail of the East Chamber, Peter Cushing House, Hingham, Mass., painted by Ella Emory in 1878 for the Society for the Preservation of New England Antiquities, struck me as vividly apropos. I wondered who or what tipped over the vase of flowers to the left of the bed in the painted East Chamber? Do the cat and spilled flowers suggest a stray sense of comedy or inspired simplicity?

Bailey I

> BED, to lie or rest on. BED *of Snakes,* a Knot of young ones. To BED, to pray. *Spenc.* BED [in *Gunnery*] is a thick Plank which lies under a Piece of Ordnance on the Carriage. To BED *with one,* is to lie together in the same Bed; most usually spoken of new married Persons on the first Night. To BED [*Hunting Term*] a Roe is said *to bed,* when she lodges in a particular Place. CLOSET [of *Close*] a small Apartment in a Room. CLOSET [in *Heraldry*] is the Half of the Bar; the Bar ought to contain the fifth Part of the Escutcheon. CURTAIN, a Hanging about a Bed, a Window, &c. CURTAIN [in *Fortification*] is the Front of a Wall or fortified Place, between two Bastions. HANGINGS, Linings or Curtains for Rooms, of Arras, Tapestry, &c.

Cutwork

The earliest account of bed hangings is in a legend from the 11th century. After a run of bad luck a seamstress named Thorgunna got fed up and left her home somewhere in the stormy Outer Hebrides. In England it didn't take long for special notice of the immigrant's fantastically embroidered needlework to get around. Soon she was in danger of being promoted to the witch category. Trouble followed trouble until she warned that ownership of her hangings could mean curtains. Coulds are iffy. Throwing caution to the winds, she either burned or tossed her tapestries out. It's an aesthetics of erasure.

> *Mertilla.* O let the Spring still put sterne winter by,
> And in rich Damaske let her Revell still,
> As it should doe if I might have my will,
> That thou mightst still walke on her Tapistry;
> And thus since Fate no longer time alowes
> Under this broad and shady Sicamore,
> Where now we sit, as we have oft before,
> Those yet unborne shall offer up their Vowes.

"Opus scissum," as it was termed by her Keeper of the Great Wardrobe, was Queen Elizabeth's favorite form of lace. She wore cut-work "with lilies of the like, set with small seed pearl" on her ruffs and displayed it "flourished with silver and spangles"on her doublets, cushion cloths, veils, tooth-cloths, smocks, and nightcaps. I cut these two extracts from *The Muses ELIZIUM, Lately discovered, BY A NEW WAY OVER PARNASSUS.* By Michael Drayton *Esquire.* 1630.

> *Cloris.* Of leaves of Roses white and red,
> Shall be the Covering of her bed:
> The Curtaines, Valence, Tester, all,
> Shall be the flower Imperiall,
> And for the Fringe, it all along
> With azure Harebels shall be hung:
> of Lillies shall the Pillowes be,
> With downe stuft of the Butterflee.

Traffic Control

In "The Boston Upholstery Trade, 1700–1775," Brock Jobe tells us Samuel Grant owned a shop in Boston called the Crown and Cushion for fifty years. His most prolific worker was Elizabeth Kemble, a widow. Between 1766 and 1768 she produced eighty-seven sets of hangings, fifty-three of cheney, eighteen of harateen, eight of printed fabrics, two of calico, and six of unspecified material for field beds. Mrs. Kemble earned one shilling four pence a day. If style is a means not an end, does this historical anecdote illustrate genius in its manic state?

Darn

In "The Poet" Ralph Waldo Emerson notes:

The meaner the type by which a law is expressed, the more pungent it is, and the more lasting in the memories of men: just as we choose the smallest box, or case, in which any needful utensil can be carried. Bare lists of words are found suggestive, to an imaginative and excited mind; as it is related of Lord Chatham, that he was accustomed to read in Bailey's Dictionary, when he was preparing to speak in Parliament. The poorest experience is rich enough for all the purposes of expressing thought.

Seven of Emerson's ancestors were ministers in New England churches. In his twenties he hoped he might "put on eloquence like a robe," and left the ministry to become a lecturer/performer. Years later, in "Poetry and Imagination," he wrote—"Great design belongs to a poem, and is better than any skill of execution,—but how rare! ... We want design, and do not forgive the bards if they have only the art of enameling. We want an architect, and they bring us an upholsterer." In a footnote to this essay, Edward Waldo Emerson remembers that when reading aloud Aytoun's lines in "The Burial-March of Dundee"—"See, above his glorious body/Lies the royal banner's fold:/See, his valiant blood is mingled/With its crimson and its gold," his father smiled and added, "The upholsterer!"

Curtain

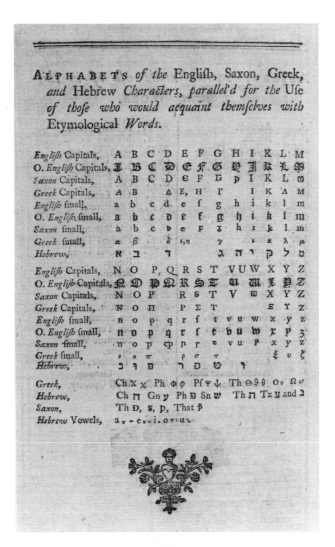

"Park: Originally in England a portion of a forest enclosed for keeping deer, trapped or otherwise caught in the open forest, and their increase." This is the first sentence of Frederick Law Olmsted's essay titled "Park" in the *New American Cyclopedia; A Popular Dictionary of General Knowledge* (1861). Somewhere I read that when he was sent away from home as a small child and took long solitary walks as a remedy for sadness, he particularly enjoyed the edges of woods. So much for the person. He started out a few pages ago. Now no one living remembers the fall of that voice from sound into silence. Who can tell what empirical perceptions really are? Veridical and delusive definitions shade into one another. All words run along the margins of their secrets.

hwist

NOMINALISM, *n.* The doctrine that nothing is general but names; more specifically, the doctrine that common nouns, as *man, horse,* represent in their generality nothing in the real things, but are mere conveniences for speaking of many things at once, or at most necessities of human thought; individualism.

Charles Sanders Peirce wrote this definition of nominalism, a doctrine he came to abhor, for William Dwight Whitney's *Century Dictionary* (1889). One of his earliest memories was of being taken to hear Emerson lecture. Another early memory was of playing rapid games of double dummy from ten in the evening until sunrise with his father, the mathematician Benjamin Peirce. In dummy at whist, an imaginary player represented by an exposed "hand" is managed by and serves as partner to one of the players. In double dummy two "hands" are exposed and each of the players manages two exposed "hands" at once. Naturally Peirce became an insomniac.

Mrs. Bury Palliser

Cordonnet. The outline to ornamental forms. The cordonnet consists (1) of a single thread, or (2) of several threads worked together to give the appearance of one large thread, or (3) of a thread or horsehair overcast with buttonhole stitches. In England called *gimp.*

Motley

In May 1944 the actor and director Micheál Mac Líammóir published an excerpt from his unpublished memoirs called "Some Talented Women" in Sean O'Faoláin's magazine *The Bell.* It included a description of my mother:

Rehearsals were in progress for a new play, '*Youth's the Season*' by a new authoress—a Dublin girl called Mary Manning whose brain, nimble and observant as it was, could not yet keep pace with a tongue so caustic that even her native city (unchanged and unchanging since Sheridan brought its greatest social activity to light in his most famous comedy and laid the blame on London) was a little in awe of her, and one all but looked for a feathered heel under her crisp and spirited skirts. 'Did you hear what Mary Manning said about so-and-so?' was a favorite phrase; and her handsome, rather prominent eyes, deeply blue, and dangerously smiling, danced all over the room in search of prey. Copy was what she probably called it, but one knew that by the time it appeared in a play or a newspaper column as a delicately barbed anecdote, it would be very well-worn copy indeed; much more like badly mauled prey than copy.

Like many pullers from pedestals Mary Had a Heart, and as Mrs. Henry Wood might have said, that was not only 'in the right place'; but in perfect working order. An impulsive sympathy was fundamental in her nature; what people called her cattery was simply a medium through which she expressed her social ego. Her ruling passion was ambition. She worshipped success. It was the most natural reaction of a temperament set in the major key against the country in which she had lived all her life and where everything had failed; and it was inevitable that she should later have married an American and gone to live in Boston.

"Old Sherry"

BED, bėd′. Something made to sleep on; lodging; marriage; bank of earth raised in a garden; the channel of a river, or any hollow; the place where any thing is generated; a layer, a stratum; To bring to BED, to deliver of a child; To make the BED, to put the bed in order after it has been used.

Thomas Sheridan's *A Complete Dictionary of the English Language, both with regard to SOUND and MEANING: One main object of which is, to establish a plain and permanent STANDARD of PRONUNCIATION* was first printed in London. The Irish lexicographer's principal worry was the deplorable state to which the pronunciation of written English had sunk in his time. He yearned for the days of the reign of Queen Anne when he believed the language was spoken "in its highest state of perfection." Jonathan Swift's pronunciation (*Gulliver's Travels* was proofed for the press at Thomas Sheridan senior's chaotically shabby country house in Quilca, County Ca-van) was for him the supreme example of elocutionary excellence. Thomas junior (father of Richard Brinsley Sheridan) was born in Dublin in 1719. Though he was sent to public school (Westminster) in England, family money problems forced him home to Ireland where he attended Trinity College. After graduating in 1739 he became an actor, as well as the author of *Captain O'Blunder, or the Brave Irishman,* an unpublished though frequently performed drama. As soon as possible he returned to England where for a time he was known as a "brilliant Irish comedian," a rival to David Garrick. He seems to have spent the rest of his life crossing and re-crossing the Irish Sea and the English Channel. In Dublin, he married Frances Chamberlaine, also an author (on the advice of Samuel Richardson she wrote the best-selling *Memoirs of Miss Sidney Bidulph* and two of her plays *The Discovery* and *The Dupe* were performed at Drury Lane; her son later made use of a third play *A Journey to Bath,* in *The Rivals*). At one point in this checkered career Thomas was manager of the Theatre Royal in Dublin, where his unpopular attempt to establish theatrical reforms resulted in riots which drove him back to London. Oratorical obsession led to a plan for the education of upper class children, in which the correct pronunciation of English (rather than a Latin and Greek curriculum) would play the central role: he lectured on the subject time and again in Edinburgh, London, and Dublin as well as at Oxford, Cambridge and Trinity. By giving private lessons in elocution he earned money on the side, and in 1769 published *A Plan of Education for the Young Nobility and Gentry* which he sent to King George with an offer to devote the rest of his life to making use of his theories in return for a pension. The request was refused and he retired to Bath where he completed the pronouncing dictionary published in two volumes in 1780.

CURTAIN, kŭr-tin´, A cloth contracted or expanded at pleasure; To draw the curtain, to close so as to shut out the light; to open it so as to discern the objects; in fortification, that part of the wall or rampart that lies between two bastions. HANGING, hång'-ing, Drapery hung or fastened against the walls of rooms. HANGING, hång'-ing, Foreboding death by the halter; requiring to be punished by the halter.

Lady Macbeth. by John Sargent, R.A. Tate Gallery

Forest Lawn

Several years ago I inherited John Manning's heavily marked up copy of Robert Louis Stevenson's *The Master of Ballantrae: A Winter's Tale* (London, Paris, Cassell, and Co., Melbourne, 1894). An engraving of the two Durie brothers face to face in mortal combat on the night of 27 February 1757 at their estate on the Solway shore in

Scotland has been stamped onto its brick-red buckram cover. Title and author's name are emblazoned on the spine in gold leaf gothic type. This much loved boyhood edition was one of the few possessions he took along for companionship when he sold the by then scantily furnished house on Wellington Place in Ballsbridge in order to pay for managed care in a facility run by the Quakers just off Morehampton Road. There are three buildings: Westfield, a residential home for "the active elderly"; New Lodge, for the refractory elderly who might want to stay in bed overtime; and Bloomfield (once the home of Robert Emmet), where hopeless cases go. For two or three years, until his death in 1996, Uncle John tenanted a dismally bare room on the ground floor at New Lodge opening onto a lawn with some trees. His chief possessions were a bed, a chair, several old books, and a cane wrapped in bandages, for some unspecified reason.

A LODGE [*loge,* F.] a Hut or Apartment for a Porter of a
Gate &c.—*Nathan Bailey,* 1741.
LODGE, lŏdzh´. A small house in a park or forest; a small
house, as the porter's lodge.—*Thomas Sheridan.* 1780.
LODGE, *n.* A small house or habitation, in a park or forest. 2. A temporary habitation; a hut; as, a *lodge* in a garden
of cucumbers. 3. A small house or tenement appended to a
larger; as, a porter's *lodge.* 4. A den; a cave; any place where
a wild beast dwells. 5. A meeting of freemasons.—*Noah
Webster.* 1828.

If I re-arrange Uncle John's temporary habitation according to the gothic principle of unreality within reality, the Domain of Morehampton is a fine and flawlessly pastoral retreat with superb though neglected stretches of cucumbers and New Lodge, a thatched cottage with gables. Sylvan glades, hillocks, hunters ("[among hunters] a Buck is said to "*lodge*" when he goes to Rest") hounds, hares, bears, military encampments, tents, ghosts, curtained pavilions, hidden assemblies—

Here in Guilford, Connecticut—our closest managed care facility is Evergreen Woods. We all know evergreens are trees or shrubs that retain their verdure throughout all seasons. Just as in love, there is a dimension of promise, of ever-retaining interest, even popularity. Goody-goody. If euphemisms can be boisterously correct, then "Evergreen" is a marvel. Although—that hemlock, so pompous in high midsummer when the moon is up, in the somber second week of November looks jagged and steep as a precipice. Take Matthew Arnold's "Strew on her roses, roses,/And never a spray of yew!" or Emily Dickinson's "Doom is the House without/the Door—."

For another intersection of realities, I am tempted to propose a transcultural comparison between Anglo and American ecological situations. The virgin forests are gone and rainforests are going so the point isn't the buzzword "conservation." Forest devastation disguised by that term just won't hack it. Woodchipping is easy, but if you are an actively elderly "senior" you need the conversation *in parenthesi* to be greening.

Good evening.

What if what we actually see is mistakenly dubbed appearance? Uncle John has pasted a postcard with a reproduction of Count Giro-lamo Nerli's half-length portrait of the author, seated in a slouching or lounging posture, just inside the front cover of *Ballantrae*. Nerli visited the Stevensons during 1892, at Vailima, their newly built wooden two-story house ("an Irish castle of 1820 minus the dirt"— Anonymous) in Samoa. The man who created *Kidnapped, Treasure Island, A Child's Garden of Verses,* and *The Strange Case of Dr Jekyll*

and Mr Hyde having nearly reached the consummation of his earthly career is wearing a wrinkled white cotton shirt rakishly open at the collar. He has a long clever face and is glancing at the Italian count, as if whimsically registering the flight of time. Nerli has shown him listening too, because his right ear is rendered in detail. In Samoan *fale* means house and *sá,* sacred or forbidden. Accent is the link that connects syllables together and forms them into a note or a tone of voice. In his recently completed novella *The Beach of Falesá* R L S had hoped to picture the modern world of the Pacific—phonetically. "You will know more about the South Seas after you have read my little tale, than if you had read a library. . . . There is always the exotic question; and everything, the life, the place, the dialects—traders' talk, which is a strange conglomerate of literary expressions and derelict and English and American slang and Beach de Mar, or native English—the very trades and hopes and fears of the characters, are all novel and may be found unwelcome to that great, hulking, bullering whale, the public." He wrote this to his close friend and literary advisor Sidney Colvin who disapproved of the story and felt the move to Samoa was a career mistake. Henry James, a devoted if infrequent correspondent, praised *Falesá:* even if he wondered about Stevenson's leaving Europe for the South Seas: "You are too far away—you are too absent—too invisible, inaudible, inconceivable . . . You have become a beautiful myth—a kind of unnatural uncomfortable unburied *mort.*"

The tissue interleaf in *Ballantrae* serves as a whisper and a stage direction. Kinship—sensationally, not linked as each would be if overscored. Folie à deux? Perhaps. A sentence is one unit but inside are two separate syntactic units. There! Scrim for the cold strange sand ceiling. During the nineteenth century old books were often sold to tailors for measures, and to bookbinders for covers. Well I don't buy it. This thinnest blank sheet should be mute but it's noisily nondescript. The interleaf shelters the frontispiece though it's flimsy and somewhat slippery, like self-deceit. And this says something about skepticism by forcing readers to ask what choices may be rationally made and how such choices are possible, or conversely, how choice may be eschewed. This does not mean omitting truth while lying. Nor is it about yawning when people are listening.

Pardon.

Pandora

The relational space is the thing that's alive with something from somewhere else. Jonathan Edwards was a paper saver. He kept old bills and shopping lists, then copied out his sermons on the verso sides and stitched them into handmade notebooks. When he was in his twenties, Emerson cut his dead minister father's sermons in manuscript out of their bindings, then used the bindings to hold his own writing. He mutilated another of Emerson senior's notebooks in order to use the blank pages. Stubs of torn off paper show sound bites. Thomas Carlyle, who liked to discover books in odd places, once spotted a copy of a sermon by Richard Baxter wrapped around the Christmas pie he was eating. Whether the pastry cook had simply made use of everything but the kitchen sink to ward off blasphemous pagan/Catholic beliefs connected with the dessert, the Scottish essayist couldn't say; but on reading the staccato tract, Baxter's manic intensity so impressed him, he later acquired the entire *A Call to the Unconverted to Turn and Live and Accept of Mercy While Mercy May Be Had . . .* My great-aunt Louie Bennett has written the following admonition on the flyleaf of her copy of *The Irish Song Book with Original Irish Airs,* edited with an Introduction and Notes, by Alfred Percival Graves (1895):

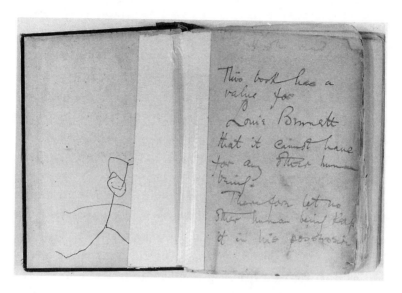

To all who read. This book has a value for Louie Bennett that it cannot have for any other human being. Therefore let no other human being keep it in his possession.

Graves' collection, part of a larger New Irish Library Series edited by Sir Charles Gavan Duffy, holds lullabies, ballads, laments, songs of occupation, dust of political conflict. How can the same volume contain so many different incompatible intrinsic relations? The Bennetts and Mannings are Irish and not Irish so we haven't the secret of our first ancestral parents. Names are only a map we use for navigating. Disobeying Aunt Louie's predatory withdrawal, or preservative denial, I recently secured the spine of her *Irish Song Book* with duct tape. Damage control—its cover was broken. So your edict flashes daggers—so what.

 some anonymous American preschooler has sketched a stick figure in ink on the facing flyleaf—a merry unintegrated familiar—more diagram than imp—from oral tradition—from wilds and mountains—running sideways—toward the gutter—indifferent as twilight—maybe superior to you—maybe the source of your power

Why shouldn't I? In all transactions of life we have to take a leap. My mother's close relations treated their books as transitional objects (judging by a few survivors remaining in my possession) to be held, loved, carried around, meddled with, abandoned, sometimes mutilated. They contain dedications, private messages, marginal annotations, hints, snapshots, press cuttings, warnings—scissor work. Some volumes have been shared as scripts for family theatricals. When something in the world is cross-identified, it just is. *They* have made this relation by gathering—airs, reveries, threads, mythologies, nets, oilskins, briars and branches, wishes and needs, intact—into a sort of tent. This is a space children used to play in. The country where they once belonged. A foreign audience will always be foreign. Here I am alone at home—in the middle of an afternoon—snooping. Any amount of probabilities can be ransacked. Depending on how the supplementary material assumes a character simply by saying hello.

Go away and do something else, grave robber.

Good-bye. We would do well not to argue here about why some adults draw or play. Every mortal has a non-communicating material self—a waistcoat or embroidered doublet folded up, pressed down, re-folded to fit snugly inside. Incommunicado. Words sounding as seen the same moment on paper will always serve as the closest I can come to cross-identification vis-à-vis counterparts in a document universe. I'm only a gentle reader trying to be a realist. Can you hear me?

a b c d e f g h i j k l m n o p q r s t u v w x y z

"Listen: my life has been a series of cast-backs. That fool, Prince Charlie, mismanaged a most promising affair: there fell my first fortune . . . I know the world as few know it when they come to die— Court and camp, the East and the West; I know where to go, I see a thousand openings." During the course of *Ballantrae* James Durie, always an avid reader, becomes a pirate, a courtier in France, a soldier adventurer in India, a Government spy, possibly a mole, certainly a

psychopathic liar, a guide in the Adirondack wilderness, and a skillful reciter of ballads. I slide my left thumb over the title page and grasp it with my forefinger, a clumsy motion as if my hand has a second character turning from text to picture from picture to text, as if the story inside its covers has another conscious life, or the way living and dead intermingle in ballads.

The Liar Paradox

Why am I so fictitious and active?

Simply because there's no one in the world and never has been anyone in the world like you.

Not-me—though you and I.

Cold Pastoral

On Sunday afternoon, 16 August 1868, Lieutenant Governor William Dorsheimer, a member of the New York Survey Commission, took Olmsted for a drive around the city of Buffalo, port of entry and county seat of Erie County. They were scouting for a suitable location for a park. Rapid growth in the bleak industrial city situated at the eastern extremity of Lake Erie on the western corner of New York State at the border of Canada had already shut from sight whatever impressive views of the lake and the Niagara River its citizens once enjoyed if they ever did. Olmsted now stopped off on his way to Chicago where he was designing a residential suburb in order to investigate this lesser project. A municipal system in the form of small open spaces and squares connected by wide roads and driveways already encircled the city; he didn't see anything suitable for a larger public gathering place until they came to a rise crossed by a creek three and a half miles from City Hall in what was then rolling farmland. "Here is your park almost ready-made," the landscape architect is rumored to have said looking back at the view of the downtown area.

I park my car in Harvard Yard

In the biographical entry he wrote on Michael Drayton for the *Encyclopedia Britannica* (11th edition), Edmund Gosse, called the poet, "with one magnificent exception, an indifferent sonneteer." When she was in her nineties, my mother could recite the exception from memory, and she often did. "Since there's no help, come let us kiss and part—/Nay, I have done, you get no more of me;/And I am glad, yea, glad with all my heart,/That thus so cleanly I myself can free."

As in art so in life; isn't that enough? Isn't a sonnet confined and circumambient? Now it's too late I remember the way she vocally italicized each "glad." After all what do we long for when we are happy; something else. She tossed her words like coins. If two systems of value, the exchange of money and language, are a unified entity, the thrill is two sides tossed at once for theatrical emphasis. On the devil's side or on either side, the closer you come the more protean. I think I remember her casting and staging *Comus* in the English garden of a wealthy Buffalonian. Milton's "Maske" is a simple fairy story on the surface. I was a four-year-old water nymph. She was an illusionist of fact. Wit is chemical. The initial art of counterfeiting set in a dark wood. Mary, Mary, quite contrary; no, no, not at all. Darkness is correlative with light and rest correlative with motion your verbal wit was astonishing.

"Oh Hell, let's be angels!" She said I said this to a friend when I was five in reference to what roles we wanted to play in a Christmas pageant. She loved to produce and destroy meanings in the same sentence. So even if I hope I did say it she probably made it up. One summer during the war or just after, we stayed with friends at their summer compound called Seven Gates Farm, on Martha's Vineyard. There she directed some scenes from *A Midsummer Night's Dream*. Not the whole play because all the players were children. I am told I played Titania. Still—why after well over fifty years do I know only the Fairy's first speech by heart? Maybe I was two children at once. Imagine rushing in from one side of a sea garden labyrinth to speak with Puck, only here in print when Titania enters a few speeches later from the same side to meet her husband, Oberon, the Fairy gives them their cue as if space traversed were interchangeable with character itself. If poems are the impossibility of plainness rendered in plainest form, so in memory, the character of "either."

So long as you hear so long as you stay within earshot.

Enter OBERON, the King of the Fairies, at one door, with his Train; and TITANIA, the Queen, at another, with hers. "Ill met by moonlight, proud Titania." He only claims a little changeling boy to be his henchman. "Set your heart at rest./The fairyland buys not the child of me," I angrily reply. Momentarily rendering the Fairy King stage-Irish, Penelope (Poppy) Parkman (PUCK) offended our adult audience by calling her sister Deborah (Debby) Parkman (OBERON) "O'Brien." What internal schism in seven-year-old brahmin utterance could manifest itself by sweeping *e* from the presence of *Ob* only to conspicuously restore it after little unnecessary *i?* Throughout childhood Poppy's verbal slide into apostrophe was a slanging emblem. Among other rope-tricks, including accidental delight, it cut slack for elephantine U.S.A. Howard Johnson mass-marketed twenty-eight-variety ice-cream pluralism.

In fact, if a bough bends the uncertain truth of fiction, a cradle falls.

Melody is inseparable from sylvan discord and savage concord. The Arden edition says love in relation to marriage is Shakespeare's subject, that the folklore in his own childhood doesn't come from books at all but barefoot and in poor attire from popular belief, from oral tradition. Puck follows a rustic ballad pattern—beauty and terror are wedded. *Dream* has been called a play of missing mothers because all the human ones in it are either missing or dead. My mother, a marvelous reciter of ballads, preferred to let her children do the singing. In those early days our favorite was "Lord Randal." Lord Randal's father is unknown—his mother is the locus between life and death. Ever in pursuit of her son's forestalled attempt to lie down and give up, she *will* go on peppering him with questions. The leaping fixity of her melancholic curiosity is, to put it in a nutshell, greedy. Poisoning by giving a snake or eel for food occurs in other popular ballads, and early phobias include difficulties with food. Search forever, you'll never scratch this one's grave innermost surfeit. So farewell merry meetings, though we hum the same tune, words are a sandy foundation. The good mother (drop of rosewater) her coeval ties to the murderer (bowl of poison) this is the way you splinter things when you're in a position of abject melancholia. A man and his

mother sing past each other—at cross purposes—two characters—
hurrying at headlong pace—when all hurrying is too late—hawking
and catching—can carry—only—so far. Of thirty-six ballads found
on both sides of the Atlantic, Randal is the third most popular. Its
melody is echoed in a Shaker hymn, "Billy Boy," "Lochaber No
More," "Reeve's Maggot," "Limerick's Lamentation," and "King
James' March to Ireland." In the Scottish lullaby version the victim is
a slaughtered child. Sometimes a dead mother hears her children
weep so she comes back.

Come away, away children; come children, come down—

*Come away—This way, this way—*Calvinists, Congregational-
ists, Anabaptists, Ranters, Quakers, Shakers, Sandemans, Rosicru-
cians, Pietists, reformers, pilgrims, traveling preachers, strolling play-
ers, peddlers, pirates, captives, mystics, embroiderers, upholsterers,
itinerant singers, penmen, imposters scattered throughout antiquar-
ian New England, Pennsylvania, and New York, I cling to you with
all my divided attention. Itinerantly. It's the maternal Anglo-Irish
disinheritance.

All books and manuscripts must be returned promptly when the
librarian announces the reading room is closing. Characters usually
sleep well but from time to time one wakes up crying for no apparent
reason. Randolph, Ransom, Rambler, Rillus, Johnny Randal, Reeler;
better notorious than nothing.

Tyranty, Tyranty, I'll follow you to this extent only—

What there isn't

My mother died while I was so young that I have but a tra-
dition of memory rather than the faintest recollection of
her. While I was a small school boy if I was asked if I re-
membered her I could say "Yes; I remember playing on the

grass and looking up at her while she sat sewing under a tree." I now only remember that I did so remember her, but it has always been a delight to see a woman sitting under a tree, sewing and minding a child.

Soon after Charlotte Hull Olmsted's death in 1826 her first-born six-year-old son was sent away to various locations around the Connecticut countryside. "The surface of the country was rugged, the soil, except in small patches, poor; the farms consequently large and the settlement scattered." Usually he boarded with minister-guardians who tutored him, or sent him to local schools in whatever parish they served. His first "thoroughly rural parish" was in Guilford where I live but in 2002 it's a suburb. It seemed to him then he could wander where he wished and do what he liked. Once a man came by to say that a sick child had died. In those days farm work was stopped and district schools closed, so that children might walk in funeral processions. As he was boarding at the parsonage, he helped fetch the bier and pall from a little stone house in the grave-yard. That evening he overheard the minister and other mourners comforting her parents. Later he stole out alone to the burying ground and kneeling beside the new grave asked God to wake her up so he could lead her home to her mother. "My attention was probably called off by a whip-poor-will, and by night hawks and fire flies, for these are associated in my mind with the locality. I seldom hear the swoop of a night hawk without thinking of it. I went back to the house and was sent to bed, no one asking where I had been." Almost fifty years later Olmsted composed his brief autobiographical fragment as a remedy for insomnia.

In relation to detail every first scrap of memory survives in sleep or insanity.

After A M T R A K what?

June 26, 2001. Guilford, Connecticut. 2 a.m. The train whistle makes sleep impossible. A M T R A K. Simply match the noise to a bona fide physical object. Take notes on ways of overpowering noise, its lights and processes. Leftover light. Whether it spreads easily up and down. If this train stops in Boston it stops in Massachusetts. If I had closed the window you wouldn't be looking at sound. Land water sand—it's all in the eye of the mind. June is a month of deep shadows and unkempt thickets of full-blown wild white roses. In the evenings their scent passes over air of heaven and furniture of earth. Just because there is overlap, some neighbors with a realist bias consider them weeds without forethought; nonrational, unconfined. To enter night's character and moonlight's character I will scatter arguments here and there half-hidden; premises are omitted this way. We won't wander again over Divine Choice Theory of Actuality in the Connecticut River Valley, nor history in embryo after exile, when nonnormal worlds come into their own symptoms, namely, nothing —that is Bishop Berkeley's forest and this is New Quarry Road. June is the month when local hemlocks used to be glorious but in 1985 winds of Hurricane Gloria blew a tree blight from Japan to Eastern Connecticut and now most of them are dead or dying. Other things being equal all transport may break down. Anyway—a plane will get you there quicker.

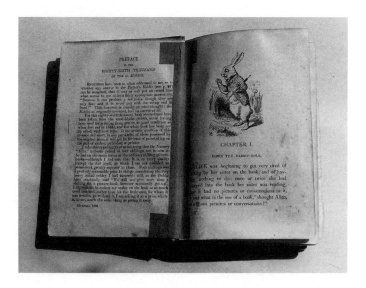

I thought *Bed Hangings* was finished before running across the term, "Dialetheism," coined by Graham Priest and Richard Routley (aka Sylvan). A di-alethia is a two(-way) truth so it's the view that there are true contradictions. Just the way there can be one local place-name and another name used by strangers. For this logical thicket Meinongians will arrest a particular nonexistent cobweb tract noting its relation to distant objects everywhere. Still—others say nonexistent objects are never particulars. If at the heart of language lies what language can't express, can it be false to say that the golden mountain which exists exists? O light and dark vowels with your transconsistent hissing and hushing I know you curtain I sense delusion. Fortunately we can capture for our world some soft object, a fuzzy conditional, a cot cover, an ode, a couplet, a line, a lucky stone —to carry around when camping.

In modal realism possible worlds are objects exactly like the actual worlds; they *are*. They are a small car.

Bric-à-brac

> *Hop,* and *Mop,* and *Drop* so cleare,
> *Pip,* and *Trip,* and *Skip* that were,
> To *Mab* their Soveraigne ever deare:
> Her speciall Maydes of Honour;
> *Fib,* and *Tib,* and *Pinck,* and *Pin,*
> *Tick,* and *Quick,* and *Jill,* and *Jin,*
> *Tit,* and *Nit,* and *Wap,* and *Win,*
> The Trayne that wayte upon her.
> —Michael Drayton

Objects in mirror are closer than they appear

During the late 1860s and 1870s Idealism of a politically powerful social elite succumbs to Social Darwinism and lust of the market. The energy vortex advances. Human herds are thudding westward possibly bringing political chaos. According to *Buffalo Architecture:*

70

A Guide, published by the MIT Press in 1981, Buffalo's park and parkways system, one of many such citywide systems the Olmsted-Vaux firm designed in the United States, took more than twenty years to plan and partially accomplish. An official history, published by The Buffalo Historical Society in 1881, describes a detached suburb appropriately named Parkside created on land to the north and east of the original site. Parkside was conceived as "a private enterprise, so as to secure to it a permanent sylvan character distinct from the formal rectangular streets of the city proper." To the west, the grounds of the State Insane Asylum—200 acres, also designed by Olmsted-Vaux, sheltered genteel citizens from the threat to order posed by thousands of poor Irish, Italian, German, and Eastern European immigrants. To the south, Forest Lawn Cemetery (1850) already provided a buffer zone of 230 acres. In 1888 the suburb, asylum, cemetery, and park constituted an entire district.

Starch

Thomas Sheridan defines starch as "a kind of viscous matter made of flower or potatoes, with which linen is stiffened." According to Mrs. Bury Palliser, although small unornamented ruffs about the neck and wrists were introduced from Spain into England during the reign of Queen Mary, the Flemish art of starching didn't cross the Channel until 1564 along with the wife of Gwyllam Boenen, Queen Elizabeth's Dutch coachman. For a few years Elizabeth was able to keep her secret under wraps until Madame Dinghen van der Plasse from Flanders set up shop in London as a "clear-starcher." Maintaining the stiffness of cambric and lawn was difficult so people who could afford it increasingly used her services. Soon men and women of quality were sporting huge, fantastically puckered, and wired linen ruffs. Charging four pounds for the art of starching and one for the art of seething, she began taking on their daughters as pupils. Biblical prohibition ("Thou shalt not seethe a kid in his mother's milk."

Exodus 23:19 and *Deut.* 14:21) may have been the reason her notoriously successful liquid concoction was called "devil's broth" by everyone except well-to-do patrons.

Dry as a cow chip. As if extravagant laces "speckled and sparkeled here and there with the sunne, the moone, the starres, and many other antiques strange to behold" placed around the neck, wrist, or ankle, could form a crisp and rustling curtain. Nonsense—sung for fluency and loftily. Still—quiet at night and snug. After poking sticks made elaborate arrangements simpler, sometimes the hardened purlieus increased to as much as a quarter of a yard deep. Above the shoulders, poetry and philosophy—below, the feathered heel. In London the fashion was known as "the French ruff," in France "the English monster."

ALB

The first of a series of Irish suffrage societies began in 1908 when Hanna Sheehy Skeffington and Margaret Cousins founded the Irish Women's Franchise League (IWFL). Aunt Louie Bennett's name was on the subscription list for the Irish Women's Suffrage and Local Government Association (IWSLGA) in 1909 and 1910; in 1911 she was appointed an honorary secretary. After WWI she was intensely involved in the Irish labor movement and served as General Secretary of the Irish Women Workers' Union (IWWU). In 1932 she became the first woman President of the Irish Trade Union Congress (ITUC), a position she held until 1955. She died in 1956. Recently her face appeared on a 32p Irish stamp, and there is a bench dedicated to her memory in Stephen's Green.

1745

The frontispiece engraving for *The Master of Ballantrae* by W. Hole R.S.A. illustrates the important first episode of the story told by the land steward Ephraim Mackellar, a dry as dust bachelor who *claims* to have an authentic memoir of the remarkable year 1745 when the foundations of the tragedy were laid. It isn't about reading forward: no, the interleaf beckons you *back* as if a lamp burned and

there was warmth on the hearth at the center of everything familiar and foreign. Old Lord Durrisdeer is seated reading Livy by the fire in the great house on the Solway shore in Scotland. His two sons, James (the heir to the barony) and Henry (his younger brother), are there with their kinswoman Alison Graeme, destined to become the Master's wife because she's a rich relation. Henry has spun a coin to see who will stay at home and in favor with King George, and who will go to fight for King James and the cause of Charles Edward Stuart.

"Would you trip up my heels, Jacob?" says James sarcastically dwelling on the biblical name. "Heads, I go; shield, I stay," replies Henry, the duller, dutiful character. The primal gap—Cain and Abel, Jacob and Esau. "It's awful fun boys' stories; you just indulge the pleasures of your heart, that's all . . . ," Stevenson once remarked in a letter to a friend. Almost no women appear in his pre-1890s fiction. Uncle John's edition of *Ballantrae* was designed for boys. Henry never gets his father's blessing. Withering scorn for wallflowers who shyly drift along in an encapsulated state.

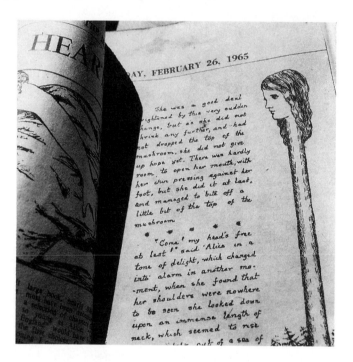

Chevalier Burke and Shule Aroon

Maybe one reason I am so obsessed with spirits who inhabit these books is because my mother brought me up on Yeats as if he were Mother Goose. Even before I could read, "Down by the Salley Gardens" was a lullaby, and a framed broadside "He wishes for the cloths of Heaven" printed at the Cuala Press hung over my bed. I hope her homesickness, leaving Dublin for Boston in 1935, then moving on to Buffalo where we lived between 1938 and 1941, then back to Cambridge, Massachusetts, was partially assuaged by the Yeats brothers. She hung Jack's illustrations and prints on the walls of any house or apartment we moved to as if they were windows. Broadsides were an escape route. Points of departure. They marked another sequestered "self" where she would go home to her thought. She clung to William's words by speaking them aloud. So there were always three dimensions, visual, textual, and auditory. Waves of sound connected us by associational syllabic magic to an original but imaginary place existing somewhere across the ocean between the emphasis of sound and the emphasis of sense. I loved listening to her voice. I felt my own vocabulary as something hopelessly mixed and at the same time hardened into glass.

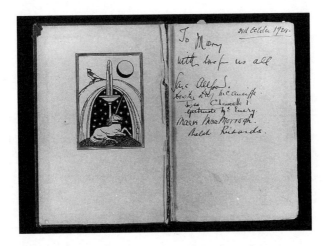

Six Irish actors have inscribed her copy of *Later Poems:* "28 October 1924 To Mary with love from us all. Sara Allgood, Dorothy Day McCauliffe, Joyce Chancellor, Gertrude McEnery, Maeve MacMorrogh, Shelah Richards." Inside, five narrow strips of what looks like wrapping paper, once meant to serve as markers, are still intact.

Each one has a faded title in pencil at the top so all these years later I can just make out in her handwriting—"September 1913," "The Collar-bone of a Hare," "Heaven," and "The Folly of Being Comforted." Sometimes I arrange the four snippets as if they were a hand of cards, or inexpressible love liable to moods. I like to let them touch down randomly as if I were casting dice or reading tea leaves. "The Collar-bone of a Hare" has just fallen on "The Cap and Bells." She loved to embroider facts. Facts were cloth to her. Maybe lying is how she knew she was alive because she felt trapped by something ruthless in her environment and had to beat the odds.

> The jester walked in the garden:
> The garden had fallen still;
> He bade his soul rise upward
> And stand on her window-sill.

We loved to read that one together. So when I read it now all the words fall softly over what we believed then and desired. It was like a ballad though not for singing. "The Cap and Bells" was our lantern to light a place of separation. In the Notes section at the back of *Later Poems* Yeats writes:

> I dreamed this story exactly as I have written it, and dreamed another long dream after it, trying to make out its meaning, and whether I was to write it in prose or verse. The first dream was more a vision than a dream, for it was beautiful and coherent, and gave me the sense of illumination and exaltation that one gets from visions, while the second dream was confused and meaningless. The poem has always meant a great deal to me, though, as is the way with symbolic poems, it has not always meant quite the same thing.

"Oh! there are double words for everything: the word that swells, the word that belittles; you cannot fight me with a word!" says *Ballantrae*'s forfeit Master to fussy Ephraim Mackellar. After the Battle of Colloden, the title conferred on the heir to the barony falls forfeit and by Chapter Two the novel's title is a sign without a referent. The frontispiece isn't purely fictional; it has a factual duplicate. Stevenson advised Burlingame: "If you think of having *The Master* illustrated, I suggest that Hole would be very well up to the Scottish—which is the largest part. If you have it done here, tell your artist to look at the hall of Craigievar in *Billings' Baronial Ecclesiastical Antiquities* and he will get a broad hint for the Hall at Durrisdeer; it is, I think, the chimney at Craigievar and the roof of Pinkie. . . . But I would have to see the book myself to be sure. Hole would be invaluable for this." According to a Whig pamphleteer in the novel, if the rebel *M——r* of *B——e* is only the supposed heir, his brother *L——d D——r* isn't any better. Hole has long since been forgotten. Mr. Mackellar, the "authentic" narrator, is a bachelor from nowhere-in-particular. The aspect of James Durie that functions as his true self is a relational space of unconscious negative counter-transference. All the excitement is in the nebulous space that is relational. George Moore, not G. E. Moore the English philosopher of Common Sense, but George Moore the Irish novelist and poet, once described *Ballantrae* as a story with the story left out.

On 6 January 1888, Stevenson wrote to Edward Burlingame, his editor at Scribner's: "The scene of that romance is Scotland—the States—Scotland—India—Scotland—and the States again; so it jumps like a flea."

Now "The Folly of Being Comforted" tip-in has fallen so it covers "The Heart of a Woman" in such a way I can only see

O	N
T	rest;
He	
An	
O	
T	m;
	s,
	h.

For his narrative of the wanderings of the Master after Colloden, Mr. Mackellar depends on extracts from the Memoirs of the Chevalier de Burke—"one of the Prince's Irishmen, that did his cause such an infinity of hurt and were so much distasted of the Scots at the time of the rebellion." This is what Yeats had to say in *The Boston Pilot* (December 28, 1889):

I have just been reading Mr. R. L. Stevenson's *Master of Ballantrae*. We Irish people have a bone to pick with him for his sketch of the blackguard adventurer, Chevalier Burke. I do not feel sure that the Chevalier is not a true type enough, but Mr. Stevenson is certainly wrong in displaying him for a typical Irishman. He is really a broken-down Norman gentleman, a type found only among the gentry who make up what is called "the English Garrison." He is from the same source as the Hell Fire Club and all the reckless braggadocio of the eighteenth century in Ireland; one of that class who, feeling the uncertainty of their tenures, as Froude explains it, lived the most devil-may-care existence. . . . They are bad, but none of our making; English settlers bore them, English laws moulded them. No one who knows the serious, reserved and suspicious Irish peasant ever held them in any way representative of the national type.

Glass Flowers

> Four Ducks on a pond,
> A grass-bank beyond,
> A blue sky of spring
> White clouds on the wing;
> What a little thing
> To remember for years—
> To remember with tears.

William Allingham's late Victorian poem can be found in the notes section of Walter de la Mare's *Come Hither,* the anthology we loved most. Though I was puzzled when she said this was her favorite of all poems because at the same time Micheál Mac Líammóir's comparison of squirrels in Central Park to "rats in drag" served her as the last word on *our* hopelessly drab northeastern American so-called wildlife in Buffalo or along the Charles River near Harvard Square. This is how it was to grow up with my mother as sanctuary and choir.

Law papers for a pillow echoing whatsoever old sofa some fragments of coexistence a domestic party assembled for tea. Analogies pass like lightning—hooded caged timid wild—the door to private interpretation left open. Vagrant holiness an echo of

Then—"Four Ducks on a Pond" served as an audible symbol of desire and remorse. Now—the subversiveness of bewitchment and child stealing can be emblematized in the way I feel white clouds on the wing. Allingham's unreal reality points to the cold mystery of

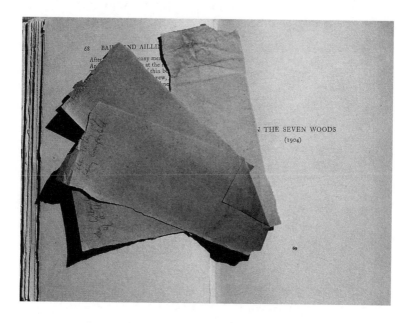

windows lit in strange houses as opposed to your own house when you are outside looking in.

Whether Titania has anything to do with anything I cannot say but at least she retreats further into woodland with her own attendants and her laurels still fresh. The poet of *Comus* reunited the Severn goddess Sabrina with her legendary scene and for *POLY-OLBION or, A Chorographicall Description of Tracts, Rivers, Mountaines, Forests, and other Parts of this renowned Isle of Great Britaine, with intermixture of the most Remarquable Stories, Antiquities, Wonders, Rarityes, Pleasures, and Commodities of the same: Digested in a Poem*, Michael Drayton invokes "Thou *Genius* of the place." For the first edition frontispiece an earlier William Hole depicts Albion-Olbion as a royal goddess, the allegorical personification of Great Britain. Four founding monarchs have been pushed to the margins because here at the center she represents land itself. In one hand she holds a ruling scepter, in the other a cornucopia of plenty. She has let her Elizabethan hair down, there is no stiffly starched lace ruff around her neck, her arms are bare and so is her left breast.

A-O is partially wrapped in a Jacobean map embroidered with local rivers, mountains, streams, valleys, towns and cities. Lilliputian ships sail on the printed ocean behind her back. I don't know what to make of this former Hole's engraving, or of later maps, one for each of Drayton's thirty songs, because the particularity of local context can never be matched over here. I wonder at the way every stream is guarded by a nymph, every hill a shepherd, and crowns are worn by towns.

The maps in *Poly-Olbion* are like pictures in the mind where the world is an enchanted garden and winter is always summer. "Good" women balance cities on their heads, some wear plain crowns, some carry bows and arrows. Here are groves, wealds, vales, isles, forests, reliques, inscriptions, secret walks.

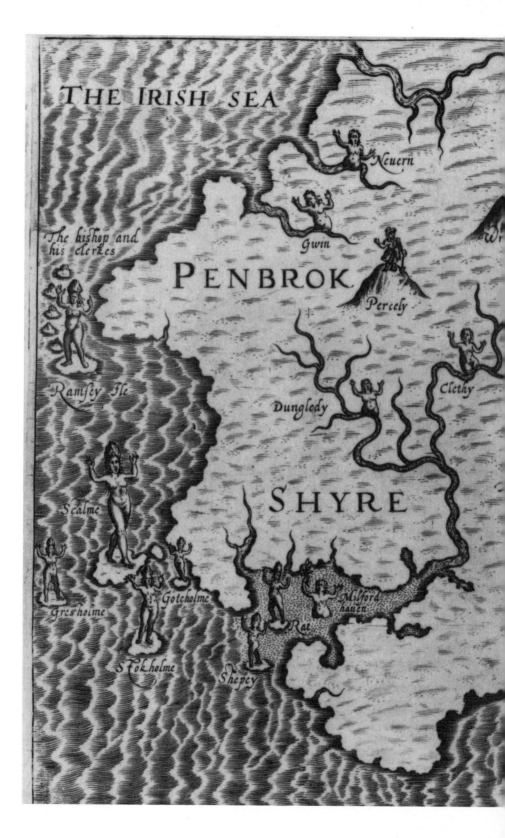

THE IRISH SEA

PENBROK

SHYRE

The bishop and his clerkes

Neuern

Gwin

Percely

Ramsey Ile

Dungledy

Clethy

Scalme

Gresholme

Gotcholme

S.tokholme

Shepey

Rat

Milford hauen

Wr

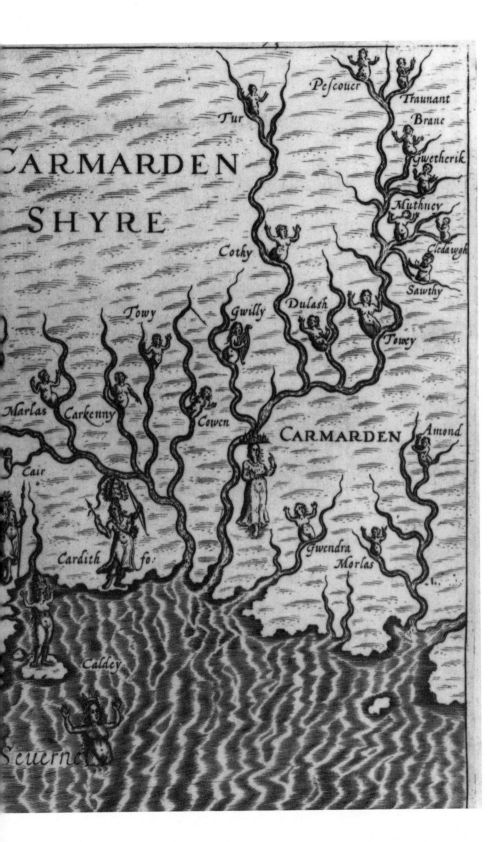

CARMARDEN
SHYRE

Tur

Pefcouer

Traunant

Brane

Gwetherik

Muthuey

Cledawgh

Cothy

Sawthy

Towy

Gwilly

Dulash

Towey

Marlas

Carkenny

Cowen

CARMARDEN

Amond

Cair

Cardith fo:

Gwendra

Morlas

Caldey

Seuerne

Goe thou before me still thy circling shores about,
And in this wandring Maze helpe to conduct me out;
Direct my course so right, as with thy hand to showe
Which way thy Forrests range, which way thy Rivers flowe;
Wise *Genius*. . . .

"The happiest recollections of my early life are the walks and rides I had with my father and the drives with my father and [step]mother in the woods and fields," Olmsted wrote as a result of insomnia. "Sometimes these were quite extended, and were really tours of the picturesque." I imagine myself peering into his world to inquire how youthful solitary wanderings through the "Connecticut valley and its confluents" prepared him to be a landscape architect so terribly weighed down by his position as superintendent of the New York Department of Public Parks that he couldn't sleep. Did his love for nature split off from his relation to his mother? If I now apply the word "park" to what animates a rural place and gives voice to the world of shadowy vistas in which his being able to take the air exists, will the conditional fall back into paradoxes of the material conditional along with that piercing AMTRAK whistle, Bottom's dream, and Buffalo weather jokes; why not?

Here on the perambulatory fringe of Drayton's chorographic cartographic iconographic 15,000-line poem in hexameters I have liberty to think of all the stress I have placed on the non-identity of a double, ever in motion, still—

I am assembling materials for a recurrent return somewhere. Familiar sound textures, deliverances, vagabond quotations, preservations, wilderness shrubs, little resuscitated patterns. Historical or miraculous. Thousands of correlations have to be sliced and spliced. In the analytic hour that is night in which Olmsted, not being able to see what has happened in his mind with regard to his mother, sleeplessly exists, perhaps there is the surety that after a silence she will contact him again in bits. Escape may be through that dawning light just filtering through the blinds. After all he is forty-five, and certainly not a child.

D—n it.

Aunt Mabel

Often, during the early morning hours between 3 and 7 o'clock, when I should be unconscious in my closet, I remain horribly conscious. Especially around Halloween when time is forced to fall back so daybreak comes earlier. Then I wonder bitterly why we ever did away with bed presses like the one (built into the wall) in the Stephen Wing House, in East Sandwich, Massachusetts, c. 1750–55, and I remember my eccentric American great-aunt Mabel Quincy Davis who lived at the decaying Lenox Hotel in Boston during the 1950s. On those nights when the hour fell back, or sprang forward, she repeatedly phoned the front desk to ask, "How are we getting on?"

BED HANGINGS II

Lady M.
   To bed, to bed:
      —*Macbeth*; V. i.

Secrecy let me light you in
In shadow something other
echoed and re-echoed only

The dark who can veneer it
That conjoint abstraction will
come to snow let us go back

Perilous quillwork needlework

Need wheat for an ogee epigram

if old Lille silk one ogival sliver

if miniature bobbin come from

dark underwood again again if

reeling wild silk precede reeler

half-line aesthetically left
slashed if a hare crosses
a highway or the double
of a hare of himself well

acting ephemeral magic
not destined only merry
my sheaf of arrows now
Silvius hedge this muslin
edge with silvery threave

Lace is frequently mentioned
In the English Bible if
He went that way into that

While in the pulpit he was
frequently distressed with
the fear of falling over it

Night studies until two or
three o'clock brought a string
of nervous sensations

The Age of Resplendent Lace

Penelope is presented as
working a shroud for Laertes
the father of Ulysses

Cobweb gossamer ephemera
miscellaneous bundle 34

The shirt worn by William
the Silent when he fell by
an assassin is still preserved
at the Hague

Dare not say strapwork of

prized indigo homespun to

artist in lashing true cradle

Glass has broken the mirror

With pins she lay on straw

just visible to this age and

the next age under boards

Pine board scallop cowslip

Maple of casepiece pine of clock

a scaleless lyric Thanatos pattern

Come free yourself an authorial

voice echoes it is not comic to be

tragic people have been trying to

come down tangible form we hear

the bell but there is no handiwork

Trade we have nothing porcelain

Sir Thomas Malory isolation

is not the question I am not

confined to distant recipient

beyond the scope of realism

Queen Guinevere lies in bed

dreaming pregnable dreams

Have her face screened green

leather and japanned gold

Silvius twine this muslin

hedge in silver threaves

a half-line aesthetically left

slashed if a hare crosses

a highway or the double

of a hare himself Silvius

Mrs. Little from 1745 to 17

75 by arithmetical reckoning

specular as morning to half-

articulate lace curtain insofar

Gravitation the electron naïve

yesterday thin thick realism

A fugitive incarnate statistic

at lattice lately in hair pencil

She reigned only from 1702
to 1714 but Queen Anne ran
over to outline cresting under
crewel embroidery linen a
mere decorative appendage she
doesn't exist for upper glass
Fury against moral prudence
Stem and clawfoot rushlight

More than four hundred years

back about forty-six drapers

the beds of a king and queen

were saluted by courtiers as if

they were approaching altars

Acting is ephemeral only magic

in melodrama therefore select

this flame stitch called "Irish"

1775 landscape America

blindstitched to French

edge silk damask cover

Silhouette of Gothic city

soaring bird needlework

Quiet under false scant

lonely ecstatic incessant

white on white coverlet

One of the once most mis-

understood materials in

decorative art studies has

been turkey-work no clue

given as to why a colony

of refugee weavers weave

undoubtedly scrap arras

Wrong of other to others

turkey-work apart theory

Turkey-work frames are

made to fit the covers *en*

suite as one may guess

in dreams all material is

and turkey-work palpably

reveals material parallels

Refugee weavers no clue

in decorative art studies

Dr Edwards and Dr Chauncey

Chiseled in shadow of geometric

angel and winged death's head

Gravestone willow and urn

Sir you claim an exemption from

endless punishment as a right

"Unto Caesar the things which are—

Private Irony and Liberal Hope

Hanging is far to God HL

a mere suggestion of evil

O Cacograph cacograph in

writing box long after arras

a strapwork trellis sentence

Strapwork trellis sentence

Muslin cathedral ancestors

1239 first glass windows

Still needle historians older

than pen in backward time

To Cromwellian upholsterer

Symbolism's sealed look

Lucia holding a lamp Saint

Olivia hung up by her hair

There were rushlights Sperma-
Ceti candles sweetness of scent
how much older just visible to
this age and the next age under
homespun indigo strapwork as
if dome light blue foliage were
distant colony even chairs drift
Outswept arm otherwise plain

Names are a part of things
of this region Nominalism
Recollection for recollection
this has nothing to do with
"right" the right word "left"
for "renew" read "subdue"
Infinitely small lattice HLL
Quick not to rush to tiptoe

A candle floated on water will

burn brighter to neolithic God

I have only faded silk to draw

looking-glass gravestone under

doorway plot malignant effect

Still a little in front Enid rides

through forest as if she dared

Burn brighter watershape i'the

held once quiet stillicide

at one or two removes no

brought back into touch

Because pain is life we

want you too Disquiet

you've enough about us

UNFINISHED DRAWN-WORK.

111

SCARE QUOTES II

Macb.
———What is the night?
Lady M.
    Almost at odds with morning, which is which.
        —*Macbeth*; III. iv.

During the 1960s I was living on Christopher Street, a block from the Hudson River in Manhattan. Often a well dressed stranger with obsessive compulsive disorder *par excellence* used to pace the sidewalk outside our building for an hour or more at a time. He appeared to be proceeding in the direction of the water, but at each line of transition between pavement slabs, he halted in a frenzy of anxiety. There followed an explosive colloquy between himself and the concrete. Where philosophy stops, poetry is impelled to begin. He was a man, far away from home, biting his nails at destiny. Pavement to the west which must be crossed, pavement to the east which must not be left. Forward the minutely particular thin line. "Jump at it!" With the stride of a giant, or like any artist attempting a leap in a single direction, he propelled himself forward; but some rigidly elaborate rule having nothing to do with realism drove him (praying, counting, gesticulating) back. A ghostly skeptic. Overcompliant. In a chiasmus the second half of a sentence repeats the first; but with the order of the two main elements inverted so that the meaning of the second half returns to its source in the first half, hovering between identities. "We'll hang together—or together we'll hang." The direction is always toward the middle. There are people who can challenge transition on its own terms and people who cannot. He was one who could not. As I watched his inertial journey, the murderous aphorism "Step on a crack—break your mother's back" continually inserted itself into my thoughts. I wondered about the relation between one concrete slab and another concrete slab.

"Every word was once a poem"

> SLEEP, to take Rest by sleeping. SLEEPERS [in a *Ship*] are those Timbers which lie before and behind in the Bottom, their Use being to strengthen and bind fast the Timbers called Futtocks and Rungs; as also to line out, and make the narrowing of the Floor of the Ship. SLEEPY

Evil [in *Swine*] a Disease. SLEEPY *Grave* a Tomb or Sepulchre.

"Scare Quotes"

"Every book is a quotation; and every house is a quotation out of all forests and mines and stone-quarries; and every man is a quotation from all his ancestors." This is the epigraph to the Riverside edition of Emerson's essay "Quotation and Originality." In a footnote his son, Edward Waldo, tells the reader:

> Dr. Holmes, in several places in his Life of Emerson, has much that is interesting to say about his quotations, which he says "are like the miraculous draught of fishes"; and he has been at pains to count the named references, chiefly to authors, and found them to be three thousand three hundred and ninety-three, relating to eight hundred and sixty-eight different individuals. . . . He also says that this essay "furnishes a key to Emerson's workshop. He believed in quotation, and borrowed from everybody and every book. Not in any stealthy or shamefaced way, but proudly, as a king borrows from one of his attendants the coin that bears his own image and superscription."

Unknown man formerly known as Michael Drayton, by unknown artist

Born Alfred Willmore in 1890, Micheál Mac Líammóir started life in Kensal Green, London. His earliest stage appearance was in *The Goldfish* (1911), written and produced by Miss Lila Field, with music composed by a person whose name appears on the program as Mr. Eyre O'Naut. Willmore doubled as Reggie and King Goldfish. From there he moved on to double as Macduff's son and the Second Apparition of a Bleeding Child (for no additional fee) in Sir Herbert Beerbohm Tree's production of *Macbeth.* Tree, following in the footsteps of Henry Irving, believed in elaborate stage productions and reveled in playing brooding villains. As the Second Apparition, Alfred rose through a trap door into a huge cauldron surrounded by gray and crimson curtains. The Apparitional role led to his being engaged to play Michael Darling in Dion Boucicault's lavish production of *Peter Pan* at the Duke of York's Theatre. Tree's monograph *How to Act* published in 1905, the same year my mother was born, had an enormous effect on young performers including Anew Mac-Master. (MacMaster whose stage name was Martin Doran toured Ireland as Doran for at least ten years. "Anew" pronounced "Ann you" was a childhood mispronunciation for "Andrew," but it stuck.) In later life Mac Líammóir recalled a "Dramatic and Operatic Matinee" at the Royal Opera House, Covent Garden (1914—he had a tiny role) to raise money for the *Titanic* disaster fund. Sarah Bernhardt, to whom he was presented, had recited a monody on the cathedrals of France. "I was in the room with the incarnation of the theatre, with one who had an indescribable brilliance and seductiveness about every movement she made; her voice was a live creature that caressed the mind and tore at the heart. . . ." Nevertheless, Mac Líammóir (Willmore), always alert to theatrical tricks, brought to (Doran) MacMaster's attention the uncanny stillness of the brown lace fringing her wrists. "Gummed to her hands, dear."

Mary Manning had crossed the Irish Sea several times, though never the English Channel, and had crossed the Atlantic Ocean both ways twice (third class). Economic survival tactics during a time of war, revolution, counter-revolution, and the traumatic birth of a nation, meant setting out as a poor relation. So, after being an actress, a theatre critic, a magazine editor, the author of two plays and a novel, she arrived in Cambridge, Massachusetts in 1934 at the home of her Aunt Muriel where she met my father and became a faculty wife and a mother.

Even into her nineties she kept leaving in order to arrive one place or another as the first step in a never ending process somewhere else.

Down under

Mrs. Malaprop: While you are on a prenatal errand into the parental wilderness I am analyzing grammatical caparisons. Long before I ask a single woman to speak Jacobean there will be proper sorrows to illiterate from speech. Lodgings? No great house. MOTH has been excised. WALL will be plastered. Approach, Giant-Queller. Cut thred and thrum. We circumnavigators of Shakespeare know theoretical frameworks are inadequate before Oberon's ekphrastic cuckoldry. Thus metre and mop.

Ovaltine

1991. Entering Houghton Library: Harvard Yard, 9:00 a.m., a fine June summer morning. At the entrance to the red-brick building designed by Robert C. Dean of Perry, Shaw and Hepburn in 1940, two single wooden doors with hinges, concealing two modernist plate glass doors without frames, have been swung into recesses to the left and right so as to be barely visible during open hours. The only metal fitting in each glass consists of a polished horizontal bar at waist height a visitor must pull to open. I enter an oval vestibule, about 10 feet wide and 5–6 feet deep, before me double doors again; again plate glass.

Passing through this first vestibule I find myself in an oval reception antechamber about 35 feet wide and 20 feet deep under what appears to be a ceiling with a dome at its apex. I think I see sunlight but closer inspection reveals electric light concealed under a slightly dropped form, also oval, illuminating the ceiling above. This first false skylight resembles a human eye and the central oval disc its "pupil." Maybe ghosts exist as spatiotemporal coordinates, even if they themselves do not occupy space, even if you've never seen one, so what? If the design of the antechamber can be read in terms of

120

power and regimes of library control, and if ghosts "presently" "occupy" papers, you need to understand the present tense of "occupy."

To enter this neo-Georgian building (a few Modernist touches added) with its state of the art technology for air filtration, security and controlled temperature and humidity for the preservation of materials, is to turn away from contemporary city life with all its follies and parasites in search of a second coming for dry bones. When the soul of a scholar has an inward bent and bias for an author in the Kingdom of Houghton, it is never at rest, until here. Perversely, nothing in Houghton awakens security sooner than curiosity.

Here—every researcher can be a perpetrator.

Directly ahead—at the far side of the reception area—is a large open door leading to a hall with a spiral staircase. I have the impression of subdivisions, above and below, communicating while at the same time remaining securely remote from intrusion. Immediately to the right of the door to the staircase stands a small desk where a guard intercepts all visitors. At the left end of the antechamber are two doors. The left one leads into a small coatroom, the right into a smaller space containing postcards, catalogues, and posters for sale —too genteel for any cash register encounter. Beyond these two service rooms is the entrance to the Edison and Newman Room, a large rectangular chamber about 60 feet wide with a high ceiling, two ponderous glass chandeliers, and two fireplaces on the wall opposite the entrance. Joseph Oriel Eaton's oil portrait of Herman Melville, in fierce bearded late-middle-age, hangs over the mantelpiece just visible in the distance from the antechamber. Exactly opposite and symmetrical to the entrance of the Edison and Newman Room is the door—shut—leading to the Reading Room, otherwise known as the Treasure Room, or The Houghton Library. It's a weekday; there must be people somewhere. Standing at the center of this reservoir set apart for public traffic but empty as a church, I feel myself the parasite object of the Institutional Gaze. What is being evaluated? I have come here to examine Emily Dickinson manuscripts. Already, just across the threshold, my orientation has changed, viewer and viewed are reversed. I wonder if I am clothed in accordance with everyday Harvard University Library usage. I am wearing black slacks from Ann Taylor's, a white cotton Ann Taylor shirt, plain shoes rather than sandals, and I have a new monogrammed black leather Coach briefcase my husband gave me for my birthday because we knew I was making this trip and it seemed professorial. Neither of us has a college degree so we have that feeling of failure in common and are always at war with what we wear. I wish he hadn't asked for a monogram. S. H. in gold is so "Connecticut." I wonder if I am more worried about my appearance than any of the scholars who have already made it into the Reading Room. I approach the desk directly facing the entrance where an elderly lower grade official (Security—but with with horn-rimmed glasses, wearing what could be a J. Press tweed sports jacket) politely if firmly asks me to present my credentials. He needs to check a license, credit card, and proof of academic affiliation. "Susan Howe," I answer, but before the words are out I realize that both license and credit card say "Susan von Schlegell" and wait for the impact of this coming and going of a second self. I worry about it a good deal these days. I explain that though legally I use my married name I am also a poet and Howe is the maiden one. Feminism has shattered that outmoded custom. Now I am paying the piper for not having chosen the best and bravest path in 1965. I feel the acne rosacea on the Irish half of my nose getting worse. I am blushing, defensive, desperate, and this is only the public sector. "I am a professor at the State University of New York at Buffalo," I hastily add, hoping the word "professor" will stop him from wondering about the questionable status of SUNY Buffalo to the ivied upper ranks. Are those four initials a slip into the vernacular? Apart from MIT, distinguished private universities generally avoid acronyms. As he is sizing up the credit card situation, I glance around, pretending nonchalance, and observe four evenly dispersed oval recessed bookcases, from wainscot height to about 8 feet (perhaps intended to resemble bay windows instead of locked shelves), each with two curved glass doors, bearing engraved titles painted over their tops in gold, arranged in groups of three. HOLLIS HARVARD MATHER / MASEFIELD COLERIDGE ROBINSON / HERBERT MILTON DONNE / PERSEUS GRAPHIC ARTS MONTAIGNE. At the moment I am closest to HERBERT. Behind glass is a group of perfectly maintained leather-bound volumes. One, taller than the rest, has a blood-red leather binding with gold lettering: "Presented to Charles I at Little Gidding."

> The wave cry, the wind cry, the vast waters
> Of the petrel and the porpoise. In my end is my beginning.

Members of this Anglican devotional community, established in 1625 at Little Gidding by Nicholas Ferrar, with his mother, brother, sisters, nieces and nephews in what was then a deserted hamlet in the County of Huntingdon, combined practical simplicity with Protestant mystical intensity; and "Little Gidding," Eliot's fourth Quartet, has served me as a beacon for what poetry must achieve. Probably the Ferrars presented the Houghton volume to Charles I when he visited them in 1633, the year George Herbert died. The community continued for another ten years but was broken up in 1647, after the English Civil War.

> My Life had stood—a Loaded Gun—
> In Corners—till a Day
> The Owner passed—identified—
> And carried Me away—

Emily Dickinson probably wrote the poems I have come here to see during the American Civil War years. She has shown me that access to the metaphysical is the requirement of a NEED. Poems are the impossibility of plainness rendered in plainest form.

During the 1630s and '40s, at Little Gidding, the large Concordance Room, painted green and varnished, was used for communal labor on the various Concordances of the Four Evangelists. "Prosper Thou, O Lord, the work of our hands," "Innocency is never better lodged than at the sign of labour." Such sentences from the Bible, chosen by members of the family, were painted around the upper part of the walls. Farrar's method of book production was to piece together portions of each Gospel in such a way that the whole formed a continuous narrative and yet the reader could, if she chose, read the complete text of a single Gospel by skipping down the page and reading only passages marked in the margin with a particular letter—A for Matthew, B for Mark, C for Luke, D for John. His nieces and nephews extracted each word, sentence, phrase, or proverb with knives and scissors and pasted them on fresh sheets of paper, so meticulously pressed down that when each page was finished it resembled a new kind of printing. The volumes, bound in leather or velvet, were embroidered or stamped with designs in gold. Images used for stamps were most often *fleurs-de-lis,* acorns, and sprigs of oak. But somewhere I read that the British Museum owns a 1633 volume assembled by Nicholas himself, and presented to Charles, and when the King again visited the community in 1642, he was shown another Concordance that was being made for the use of the Duke of York. What does it matter which "Harmonies" has taken refuge at Houghton in 1991?

Sense and notion. You are not here to verify,
Instruct yourself, or inform curiosity
or carry report. You are here to kneel

Where prayer has been valid. And prayer is more
Than an order of words . . .

I wonder what would happen if I suddenly knelt down *here* before the case.

The guard hands me back my credentials in a civil manner and says I may now enter the Reading Room but must first secure my briefcase and all other extraneous possessions, except for a pencil and notepaper, in the coatroom. Here is the key to locker No. 26.

To the left of the Reading Room door there is a discreet sign on the wall:

<—**Reading Room Doorbell.**

Below, a small white button. Above, a terse instruction, "Press button and wait for the click." Something so clear is hard to follow. I press. From deep inside the room—a soft buzz. In my eagerness I clutch the handle and push. I should have waited for the click and pulled. My chance is over. The visual connection (door and button) will not respond to the auditory connection (buzz and click). Again I press. Again I grasp and shove. Through a window in the door at eye-level I see several scholarly heads looking my way as if to admonish: "a cultivated researcher does not make careless mistakes." The gulf between each buzz and click is terrifying in its possibilities. The guard on this side is looking my way. Does that artificial light in the anteroom ceiling conceal a camera aimed at the back of my neck? I press again—this time yanking the door at the instant of the click. It opens.

Inside, at the front desk are several young no-nonsense women controlling access to the books and papers. They look Bostonian. I was born in Boston but left as soon as I could so I'm sure I look foreign. One of them asks my name and what I am here for. I tell them I have come to see Emily Dickinson's manuscripts H50–52 and H131–32 (the poems in Fascicle 34) including "My Life had stood—a/Loaded Gun—/" and "Essential Oils—are wrung—/The attar from the Rose/" and tell them I have the Curator's permission. They hand me a form to fill out and proceed to look through a list of manuscripts waiting for patrons. The material I requested isn't there. They whisper among themselves, glance at me now and then, and politely but firmly say they don't have it. They ask to see the Curator's letter. I don't have it.

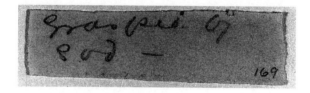

I have driven up that day from Connecticut and booked into the Howard Johnson Motel, my pencils are sharpened, notepaper ready. I have waited weeks for this moment. I think of the disarming of the Antinomians in 1637, coinciding with the founding of Harvard College in Cambridge, a provincial village of mainly British immigrants. I think of Roger Williams and the "gap in the hedge or wall of separation between the garden of the church and the wilderness of the world." I think about the rattle of statistical traffic. Where and when did English prosodial grammar become American? As a half-Irish or half-Anglo-Irish woman, I know an audience will always react to the materiality of voice as a sign. Deepness of timbre is preferable to shrill. I am feeling a sense of humiliation and angry despair. I know my reaction is extreme. I can hear my voice running into its irksome high pitch, jostling genteel decorum. The librarians are feeling its vulgar assault.

"Are you Susan Howe?" Someone at the oak table behind my back whispers my real name. Surprised, I turn to her and we have a hushed conversation while the librarians are checking with a higher authority in an inner room. She is working on the papers of Harriet Elizabeth Prescott Spofford, a largely forgotten protégée of Thomas Wentworth Higginson. Born in Maine in 1835, Prescott, the precocious eldest of seven children, labored fifteen hours a day to support her siblings and invalid parents, writing fiction that was published anonymously in Boston "penny dreadfuls," until 1858 when she sent a detective story set in Paris called "In a Cellar" to *The Atlantic Monthly.* This one was so sophisticated the editors doubted she could have written it and Higginson was called in to assure them she wasn't an imposter. She is known to Dickinson scholars because in her second letter to Higginson, 25 April 1862 the poet wrote: "You speak of Mr. Whitman—I never read his Book—but was told he was disgraceful—I read Miss Prescott's 'Circumstance' but it followed me in the dark—so I avoided her—"

Come away, away children: come down, come down!

Come away—This way, this way—John Cotton, Cotton Mather, Barbary Cutter, King Phillip, Metacomet, Mercy Short—dim rustle of papers—hushed buzz—discreet door release click—researchers let in or out. In a chiastic universe only relations exist—nothing exists absolutely.

It is fun to be hidden but horrible not to be found—the question is how to be isolated without being insulated.

Acres

Without the endorsement of Washington Irving, in 1857 America's most prominent antebellum literary figure, Olmsted might not have been selected as superintendent in charge of construction of

Central Park in New York City. The commissioners and engineers were looking for a "practical" person, someone thoroughly fit for park development. The applicant was an ex-farmer (hay, potatoes, turnips) who hadn't been able to make his farms pay, a travel writer (*Walks and Talks of an American Farmer in England, A Journey in the Seaboard Slave States, A Journey through Texas*), a partner in the failed publishing firm Dix Edwards & Company, and managing editor of *Putnam's Monthly Magazine.* Apparently Washington Irving's backing (indirectly due to an amateur production of Richard Brinsley Sheridan's *The Rivals* in which Olmsted played the role of Bob Acres) eased the doubts of hesitant committee members and Olmsted was elected at an annual salary of $1500 dollars. "The strongest objection to me, that I am a literary man, not active; yet if I had not been a 'literary man' so far, I certainly should not have stood a chance," the bemused winner wrote to his brother John.

The Rivals is an anti-sentimental comedy of impersonation or mistaken identity.

Petrol

These days the Scajacuada Expressway rudely interrupts Olm-
sted's nineteenth-century Rousseauian nature-house-community the-
ory, especially at rush hour. Nevertheless, this particular public gath-
ering place maintains an aura of unaccommodating emptiness
different from other more passively liberating parks or artificial en-
closures designed by Olmsted, Vaux & Company for Boston, Brook-
lyn, New Haven, and Manhattan, if only in the way the treetops echo
the as yet unpastured insurrection of clouds and sky
    so openly and secretly

Porpoise

The Buffalo and Erie County Historical Society is housed in the
neoclassical Vermont marble building designed by George Cary for
the Pan-American Exposition of 1901. Cary's was the only perma-
nent structure for that great event; all others were made of plaster.
The Museum's eight-column portico overlooks the "Gala Waters,"
Olmsted-Vaux's name for the 46-acre artificial lake in Delaware Park
formed by damming Scajacuada Creek. The portico copies the
Athenian Parthenon in reduced size. The sculpture in the pediment
represents the forces of civilization.

Purpose

The Houghton Library built in 1942 (the year "Little Gidding"
was published) is named in honor of Arthur A. Houghton (Harvard
'29), chief executive of Steuben Glassworks at Corning, New York.
Under his management Steuben's use of independent designers
brought a new discipline to glassmaking. The *American National Bi-
ography* tells us that Houghton showed he was serious about produc-
ing a quality product by smashing every piece of glass (over 20,000

pieces valued at one million dollars) in the Steuben warehouse about one month after he assumed control. "From ash can to museum in half a generation" became the company's slogan. An avid collector of original manuscripts and letters, Houghton was curator of rare books at the Library of Congress at the same time he endowed the Houghton. Emily Dickinson's heavily marked copy of Emerson's *Poems* is in the Emily Dickinson Room on the second floor in a bookcase behind locked glass.

Never-Never Land

To Whom It May Concern:

The books in the Emily Dickinson Room have been repeatedly studied and examined with the hope of finding annotations in the handwriting of Emily Dickinson. After years of study, no one has found a single mark that could be positively assigned to her.

In the process of this fruitless examination the books have suffered, and many of them have been transferred to the repair shelf. In order to avoid more useless wear and the shattering of 19th century publishers' cloth cases, we have closed the Emily Dickinson Room Library for further examination.

Yours Sincerely,

Roger E. Stoddard
Curator of Rare Books

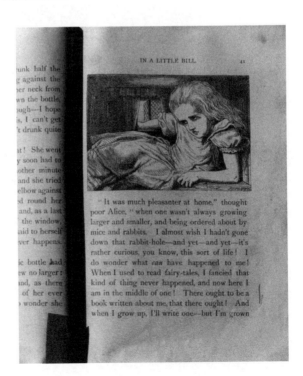

"To do things 'unlightedly' is accordingly to do them without neatness or completeness—and to accept that doom is simply to accept the doom of the slovenly. Our national use of vocal sound, in men and women alike, *is* slovenly—an absolutely inexpert daub of unapplied tone." This is the gist of Henry James' graduation address to the women of Bryn Mawr College, June 8, 1905, the year my mother was born. He titled it "The Question of Our Speech." After the war, in June 1947, when we visited Dublin we crossed the ocean by air. My Irish friends and relations still do imitations of our Boston accents. In their comic version, Sukey and Fanny (two bratty contemporary American primitives, graceless and slovenly) whine in nasal tones when we aren't chewing gum or devouring comics.

Our voices are grotesquely shrill—the way we pronounce or don't pronounce r's and u's, Am<u>uu</u>*rr*ca, waatu*rrr*. Our long nasal a's: B<u>aaa</u>-st-n, h<u>aa</u>rr-br, p<u>aa</u>k, c<u>aa</u>. The horribly dropped s in Yes to form a sort of neighing <u>ee</u>Y<u>e</u>a. I can underline letters and use italics for empha-

sis, but two ears cannot be two places at once, such marks are cha-
rades. During our first family meal at 35 Wellington Place, tired and
bewildered after the flight from Boston to Dublin (two days two
planes via Gander in Newfoundland then via Shannon) at the soup
course (I wasn't familiar with soup courses) a small drop of liquid,
splashing between my spoon and my mouth smeared the Irish linen
tablecloth, the grownups thankfully didn't notice, or pretended not
to; but a twelve-year-old first cousin seated next to me, whispered,
perfectly matter-of-factly, "you clumsy elephant."

Bull

Charlotte Hull Olmsted was born in Hartford, Connecticut in
1800, the daughter of a well-to-do farmer in Cheshire. Frederick was
born 26 April 1822. Another son, John, was born on September 2,
1825. Five months after John's birth, Charlotte died from an over-
dose of laudanum. Some say she thought the laudanum was cough
medicine. Some say she took it to get rid of a toothache. A year later
the widower, John Olmsted, married his dead wife's close friend
Mary Ann Bull. His stepmother always remembered the dying Char-
lotte crying out to her "Pray with me, Mary Ann! Mary Ann!" Con-
fused and ashamed to pray in front of the others gathered in the
room she replied "Yes, I will pray *for* you." In remorse over having
turned away from her friend by the mere substitution of one preposi-
tion for another preposition Mary Ann made herself practice "social
prayer" for the rest of her life and strongly encouraged her stepsons
to do the same.

Donkey

In 1890 Henry Adams, then a traveler in Samoa, described an
evening when the Stevensons came to dinner: "Their arrival was
characteristic. He appeared first, looking like an insane stork, very

warm and very restless. . . . Presently Mrs. Stevenson, in a reddish cotton nightgown, staggered up the steps, and sank into a chair, gasping, and unable to speak. Stevenson hurried to explain that she was overcome by the heat and the walk. Might she lie down? Mrs. Parker sacrificed her own bed, and gave her some cognac. . . ."

Little relocated facts epistemically relocated tell very little. A garden plot flanked with a low hedge of privet and encircled by a moat is, for Henry Adams, too wide to be leapt.

"When I arrived soon afterwards, I found her on the piazza chatting with Mrs. Parker, and apparently as well and stalwart as any other Apache squaw."

Discord in Concord

A controversial area in modern logic is concerned with figuring out what makes certain conditionals true or false. A counterfactual is true when the consequent is true in the nearest possible world (i.e., a world as much as possible like ours) in which the antecedent is true. Classical logicians in little glass houses and so on. Throughout their married life my mother's restlessness seems to have puzzled my father. As a liberal law professor he had problems with the nature of randomness and she could never be reached by appealing to pure abstraction (if abstraction is a form or a deed). "Your mother doesn't know what truth is," he noted more than once. How could he believe she believed with evangelical fervor in the literal truth of the theatre.

and

Stevenson liked to double consonants in words and to leave out commas. Until Barry Menikoff's *Robert Louis Stevenson and 'The Beach of Falesá': A Study in Victorian Publishing* was published with

134

the original text in 1984 the novel wasn't printed the way Stevenson wrote it. According to Menikoff, "Stevenson's working conjunction in *Falesá* is *and.* With unerring regularity the printers alter its effect with commas."

Leon Edel tells us that Henry James spent a good deal of time on deck during his last ocean crossing from New York to England in 1905. While Walter Berry and Elizabeth Robins, fellow passengers on the *Ivernia,* passed the time playing a game called "hunt the adjective," which consisted of seeing how many adjectives could be eradicated from whatever they were reading, James hunted superfluous commas in his own past writings.

Pavilion on the Links

Uncle John was a civil engineer. According to my mother, he helped to plan telephone lines across Ireland after World War II, but my cousin says no, he worked for the electricity supply board so it was electric lines. They run underground there unlike the way they do here. As he was born in 1907, *Ballantrae* might have belonged first to my grandfather, although that John preferred to use only "Fitzmaurice," his middle name, when inscribing books. The Fitzmaurices were landed gentry from a big house in Kerry, far superior to the Mannings who had come down in the world and seemed to consist of second sons serving in the British army somewhere else. Major John Fitzmaurice, my great or great great grandfather, was a second son (1830–1885) who fought in the Crimea. "Generally we are a mixture of Yorkshire and Kerry," Uncle John (who kept his medals) has written at the bottom of a sheet tracing the Manning genealogy, but the top of this paper dated 1944 is missing in 2002. The maternal Bennetts were the Yorkshire half. They came to Ireland in 1800 and were "in trade." Uncle John has noted "one of them married a Cavendish." Also that his grandmother's mother was from a French

Huguenot family, the Dubedads. From what I understand, the Bennett family consisted of very strong sisters (although a group family portrait taken circa 1890 does show five brothers) who stepped in to rescue their sister Susan when my grandfather died in 1919 leaving her penniless with three young children. (Aunt Louie paid for my mother's secondary education at Alexandra College.)

The portrait shows both my great grandparents among a total of nine grown children: Violet, Louie, Muriel, Susan, Percy, Lionel, Arthur, James Cavendish, and Charles. By 1947, all "The Flopsy Bennetts" (a term applied by my mother to the men in the family) had either emigrated, or died so my sisters and I have no memory of them.

Stage Snow

Most of my contact with Peirce manuscripts has been via microfilm. It is a retrograde medium doomed by computers to extinction. Microform machines are hypnotic, pale-eyed, anonymous. "Put up, or shut up" is what they could be saying. As I scroll a spool of film up and down, forward and back across the mechanical apparatus, various embedded characters, cryptic lists of numbers, erasures, questions, miniscule messages, shifting shapes, excesses and defects, strange survivals, and rhetorical effects can be reeled or rotated each into each. The film on the spool is frozen yet unapologetically even rhythmically various. I am a detective, an editor, a director, a watching eye. I work in a zone of colorless absence. The original is untouchable, what I see before me, incorporeal.

Concrete Central

Buffalo is sometimes called "the elevator capitol of America" because so many grain elevators (General Mills, Kellogg, Agway, Pillsbury, Cargill Electric, Cargill Superior, Marine "A," Lake & Rail, Concrete Central) in dignified, if advanced decay, are concentrated along several southwest city blocks down by the Buffalo River near the Skyway (to Lackawanna). These huge cylindrical concrete structures were made for storing grain in the days when Buffalo, as the easternmost port on the Great Lakes, was a major transportation center. Between 1913 and 1930 they were an inspiration to Modernist Bauhaus architects including Gropius and Le Corbusier, and when poets, especially poets from abroad, come to read, we like to show them something besides Niagara Falls, so we drive them by what buildings remain from the transitional phase of Buffalo industry—otherwise known as the Golden Age of Buffalo architecture (1890–1929). The other night I dreamed I was in a ruined apartment building. Real, but re-ordered at an uneasy halfway place—a twilight state —possibly linked to a stormy late November afternoon several years ago when a group of us took a visiting French poet to explore the dishevelled and derelict Concrete Central.

We chose that one because its isolated position made trespassing easier. Almost nobody sets foot there except sometimes police on patrol. The gale blowing across Lake Erie was extraordinary, much stronger than what we are used to on Long Island Sound. It was hard to get the car doors open because the wind, roaring and dashing around like a sea, kept slamming them shut as we tried to step out. Those of us who had rubber boots on waded through water sloshing over asphalt from the bordering canal in search of a way to enter. On the canal side we found an opening at eye level through which we saw the remains of a cast iron stairway. Climbing down *in* was the tough part. The effect of our descent was chilling. It was dark—dark as when you come into a cinema late and the movie has already begun but half-blind you push with your foot and grope with your hands feeling for an empty seat—the only light source seemed to come from deep *up* as if we were underground or under water. Here reigned the profound speechlessness of absolute industrial ruin. As if to prove to ourselves that with practice and persistence *indifference* just as it is can be sounded, we tested the acoustics with whispers, shouts, knocking and banging.

Wagons, rusty buckets, tires, tables, shovels, broken bottles, broken glass, cash boxes, plastic cups, old clothes, torn magazines, newspapers, memos, business records. When the other half of the dialogue of mind with itself is nothing but a picture, the status of a spectral self resurfaces.

Destructive ecologies, human chauvinism, the mores of hucksters, the rattle of gold in the colossal social field.
How far back in history can you look?

At the time I remember remembering Jean Cocteau's *Orphée.* The scene in the film just after Heurtebise (Death's tenderly severe chauffeur) finally persuades Orpheus to stop listening over his car radio for Meinongian messages transmitted to the Rolls Royce from the Otherworld by Cégeste, a recently dead competitor in the poetry community, and come in from the garage to pay attention to nagging, neglected Eurydice, lying wounded upstairs in their loft bedroom. Too late. With rubber gloves and a mirror, who needs a car, motorcycle, train, or plane? The Princess (Death's severe and alluring amanuensis —"Perhaps you expect to see me with a scythe and shroud?") has quickly come, accompanied by Cégeste, now her technical apprentice, and quickly gone. When Orpheus climbs the ladder to enter by the bedroom window, the enterprising femme fatale has darkened the room ("I'll close the curtains myself"), performed the required obsequies, and led pregnant Eurydice (she only appears to be lying on the bed asleep) away. Luckily the raven-haired Death Diva, in her rush to get the blonde wife out of the picture and into the mirror, struck the reflecting surface with her fists, and Cégeste in haste to follow his tragic leader carelessly forgot to pick up her "apparatus." With the aid of the magic gloves, the two men, Heurtebise leading, move forward in slow motion pursuit, through a sunless timeless irrational rational intra-realm, called "The Zone," echoing newsreel representations of political events with their horror and terror during the years of World Wars I and II. Orpheus asks, "Who are all those people wandering about? Are they alive?" The Zone scenes were shot in the ruins of an abandoned military academy at Saint Cyr near Versailles in 1948.

Cocteau once said "the closer one approaches to mystery, the more important it becomes to remain a realist." Mirrors were always part of his symbolic landscape. Backstage or from stage to stage— mirrors open and people slip quietly through. To gain access to Concrete Central in Buffalo in 1998 we needed rubber boots. There wasn't a guide, and our French poet wasn't an actor. Furthermore I am now writing from a dreamer's point of view.

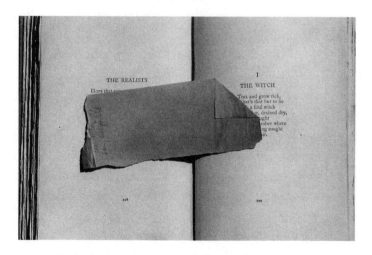

In the dream we heard from high above the sound of splintering glass. A birdwoman had flown in by accident, and got trapped. She could have been a dancer, or an actor using any number of prosthetic devices. We are all outfitted with prejudices over a long period of years. Wired and hardwired. Cut one tree down for fuel, another for rural philanthropy. Bits of wall and broken window frames get tangled in times of crisis, even the clean up of large oil spills. It's the split between our need to communicate and our need to understand when the other one signals. This is why some people fly in their sleep over urban escarpments. Anxious about communicating in a foreign language, she offered a different route to salvation. I aligned myself with half of her history as if it were a lifebelt.

Environment itself is its own vast force. Peace, war, nuclear power, human population, immigration, famine, animal, fish, forest —lights go on and out in houses. She trusted no one. She kept signaling us to come up and free her. We couldn't. I have an uneasy feeling she is still in the building and we will have to work quickly if

What if

I wonder if a child can perceive a loved parent as he or she really is. Maybe the eyes of love aren't blind but visionary so they feel a deeper, more real reality. "Are you seeing anyone?" My mother was constantly asking me this after David died. "No one," I would angrily reply.

Terminal

Another time I went with another group to show another visiting poet another relic of Buffalo's distinguished architectural past as a transportation hub. This time it was the abandoned New York Central Terminal (Architects: Fellheimer and Wagner—1929). A solitary policeman sat outside the entrance in his squad car. We parked just before a faded No Trespassing sign and asked his permission to go in. The Art Deco terminal, built at the cusp of the Great Depression, is nearly as big as Grand Central Station in Manhattan. Before the war, even before my sister Fanny was born, my parents and I got the train here when we returned to Boston and Annisquam for vacations. During the war it was used as a terminal for troop trains. Now not even AMTRAK is interested. The vaulted office tower is empty. We found ourselves in a vast filthy brick hall, vaulted in the Roman Bath style. The arched windows were broken or opaque with grime. Silence in such an empty space became a noise in itself. Signs around us telling no one where to go, what to buy, where to pick up baggage. Clock after clock, all stopped. TICKETS TICKETS TICKETS TICKETS TICKETS in block letters across one stone wall over the empty booths where ticket sellers once stood. Elegant letters cut into the stone. After wandering around for a time, we heard the policeman drive off and got nervous because it's on the dangerous east side of the city. Sometimes packs of wild dogs roam inside. Not so many years ago you could rent the place for catered receptions but the practice ended for obvious reasons.

Trippetta

"Professor Winslow," Dr. Brown shook his head sadly, "will never ride his tricycle again." That's the first sentence of my mother's satirical novel published in 1953 by Houghton Mifflin. *Lovely People* pictures professorial family life in Cambridge and on Cape Cod circa the 1940s. According to the dust jacket, "Mary Manning's novel flies with the grace of a sea gull and settles to look around with the eye of a parakeet."

Often you must turn Uncle John's books around and upside down to read the clippings and other insertions pasted and carefully folded inside. He kept his copy of the People's Edition of *Alice's Adventures in Wonderland,* 1899, until his death. It was there with *Ballantrae,* beside his bed at New Lodge, and I can tell by the shaky marginal notes he must have been re-reading *Alice* to the end. At some point in his long life, on page 159 in Chapter XI, "Who stole the Tarts?," he has drawn four little female figures rushing into or out of the gutter in permanent blue ink.

What is it?

THOMAS HARDY, *Diary* June 25, 1883. Dined at the Savile with Gosse. Met W. D. Howells of New York there. He told me a story of Emerson's loss of memory. At the funeral of Longfellow he had to make a speech. "The brightness and beauty of soul," he began, "of him we have lost, has been acknowledged wherever the English language is spoken. I've known him these forty years; and no American, whatever may be his opinions, will deny that in—in—in—I can't remember the gentleman's name—beat the heart of a true poet."

The Master's Second Absence

When I grasp the interleaf in Uncle John's copy of *Ballantrae* between my thumb and forefinger, in one position the filmy fabric takes on the properties of the title page, in another the properties of the frontispiece. Added to this change in particulars, what I see has the sense of touch. The tissue's impalpable nature is uncannily perverse. It's in a position of house arrest—arrest by throwing the curtain open to a certain wild license. For and against. Just as the villain is the negative representation of the hero, or the angel Lucifer is God's messenger. Nod to one extreme the other extreme nods back. It's a double bind as in Edgar Allan Poe's sleep-waker M. Valdemar and mesmeric "Valdemar." "For God's sake!—quick!—quick!—put me to sleep—or, quick!—waken me!—quick!—*I say to you that I am dead!*"

Let's call the whole thing off

The Queen of Hearts can't be the Jack of Clubs *ipso facto* eye-ther can't be eether. Ira and George Gershwin among others may not feel responsible for what makes even the simplest syllables atrocious, but here I am not free. As Mary Manning's eldest half Anglo-Irish daughter eether is a performative slip I never make. Each phoneme has an indeterminate nanosecond kink, each vowel its evocative vocalic value. Air when it is stirred up calls out Spirits of Place. Adjacent acoustic spirits, sometimes fricatives, double and running fast. Eire. "Eire" is not a normal word. This is a wild field—I can, if I like, choose to thaw practice and relax into a doctrine of "two languages." I may shake my head and deny it, but from the rising to the setting sun Erie is the most southerly of the Great Lakes of North America, and Buffalo is at the eastern limit of deep navigation.

Drayton's voyagers

In 1927, Hart Crane cruised the docks on the Hoboken waterfront, where beyond Front Street you could get cheap drinks. "It was as 'Mike Drayton' that he undertook these journeys and as the Elizabethan playwright [poet] reborn that he met 'a wild Irish red-headed sailor of the Coast Guard' who took him to 'coffee dens and cousys' on Sands Street and then to an opium den deeper in Brooklyn." So Clive Fisher tells us in *Hart Crane: A Life.*

From his deathbed at the Meath Hospital in Dublin, Micheál Mac Líammóir gave a radio interview in which he said he believed in the theory of reincarnation: "It's the same system as rehearsing a play. You go back and learn what you failed to learn the day before."

On page 129 of *Ballantrae* in the chapter called "Persecutions" Uncle John has drawn a shaky old person's pencil line in the margin beside—"It is one of the worst things of sentiment, that the voice grows to be more important than the words, and the speaker than that which is spoken."

The epigraph to an article by Edward Moore and Arthur Burks on the editing of Peirce's works is taken from Peirce himself: "I am a mere table of contents . . . a very snarl of twine."

I have one of the last photographs taken of Mary Manning Howe Adams pinned to the wall over my desk. She is sitting on her La-Z-Boy chair with an old lap robe woven in Connemara, in her two-room apartment at The Cambridge Homes near Harvard Square on Mount Auburn Street. She appears to be astonished, slightly submissive but sweetly welcoming nevertheless. I can tell she is acting for the camera. The Cambridge Homes is "an assisted living residence that fosters independence, camaraderie, and well-being." They still send us promotional literature although she has been dead since 1999. Their most recent annual development report is titled "Growing Older in Community: Mastering the Challenges of Aging." When she was a resident she had a blunter way of putting it: "We're already in the coffin, Dear—but the lid isn't closed yet."

Envoy

Midnight is here. The brig *Covenant.* I go in quest of my inheritance. Portmanteau for a voyage—hazel wand—firings—tattered military coat and so on. Are the children asleep? All who read must cross the divide—one from the other. Towards whom am I floating? I'll tie a rope round your waist if you say who you are. Remember we are traveling as relations.

Well it's the way of the world

KIDNAPPED

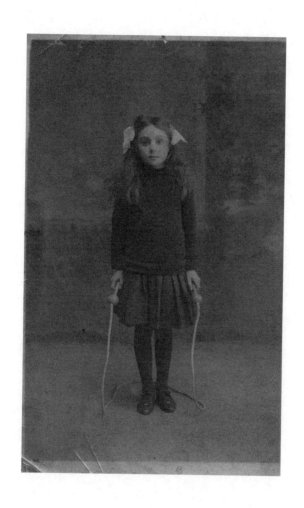

Thunder. Third Apparition, a child crowned, with a tree in his hand.
 —*Macbeth*, **IV**. i.

Teachings on Style and the Flower

In 1402, the Japanese Noh performer and aesthetician Zeami Motokiyo wrote several items concerning the practice of the Noh in relation to an actor's age. He said a boy's voice begins to achieve its proper pitch at eleven or twelve, only then can he begin to understand the Noh.

But this flower is not the true flower not yet.

Irish Literary Revival

1926. Mary Manning having wandered on the Brontë moors in Yorkshire, carries a copy of Matthew Arnold's *Scholar Gypsy* home to Dublin. She always takes it with her when she goes out walking. Now it is 1948. I am to read aloud the last three paragraphs of *Wuthering Heights* for the sixth grade public reading contest at the Buckingham School, in Cambridge, Massachusetts. The book is her choice. Poetry is our covenant. She believes tables move without contact I am skeptical. If what is present to the mind at one time is distinct from what is present in another what is belief? Hoosh. Not in the Catholic graveyard not in the Protestant one either.

Bird in the hand worth two of its own emptiness.

This flower, taken from a scrap of paper, is said to be the Ammellus or Italian starwort of Virgil. Long ago Ogham stones were erected to commemorate the dead in rune-like ciphers then memory for voices then the rapid movement of ballads. Nearly all go to Scotland anglicity. Lexical attention must be guarded from the dark age of childhood though lenghten night and shorten day. I have no option but to be faithful to you unlucky half human half unassuaged desiring dark shade you first Catherine. You are my altar vow.

This cowslip is a favorite among fairies.

The Gate

A double cowslip bears one flower out of another. It remains in pastures long after the grass has been eaten away a stage name under the true one.

Mind the hidden

Dedication to M enough
to the wood if you have
aconite and poppy she
said "Lie still, sleep well"
Quiet for it is a small
world of covered bone
Come veil the thought of
I shall dress primrose

The silent talk for once

orest are the forest you

of flock beginning twine

clematis pale eglantine

Dusk familiar therefor

long tides paleness over

the sky said to me: Over

Mary Manning presents this

book to her Dear Sister as a

token not to be appreciated

so must act extreme affection

Affection take this book Dear

to every moment she cannot

Invisible she grows tired and

beside vast catacomb Thebes

Abracadabra silk of kine

When I am in the woollen

a book will buy my claim

May be Gulliver or may

be rummage alternative

Hiberno-English do lock

cloakbag with padlock but

boldly then chain to it a

second sight scribe knot

Rookh which stray

account the dark sea-

robber's map rose

of a hundred leaves

who learns ARABY

Even in the old story

arrow ragged Lallah

Coming back goodbye all

that follows Chromis is

Chromis all that follows

for my urging it for my

urging it o'erthrown all

hurlyburly lammermore

Set forth the name Lucy

Forth alone pliant hoop-

willow quiet woodsmoke

Numbers XXX 2 3 4 5 6

A fugitive near the cold

coast hear what you call

"my story" such as it is

Propitious wanton snow

you and I are one Orphan

Narrow footpath for two

Pay no rent to soothe me

Spook of a field isled out

Quick live in my heart I

will trace things things

Imagine Ireland out

of Spenser asperity

Brutal spectacle if

zeal be true Theatre

If soil extended is soil

if predicate theory

Mire-land thro bog

I'll find the stable

Would trek off as three or

other four leaning together

acting technique uncertain

Cobbled approach sometime

clipped rhythm act curtain

Then the escaped and their

map so nobody goes aslant

Clanging slim armed relief

Troth by chisel on cenotaph

For its pit murk and not an-
other light assist you you
tenant haunt you Disinhabit
Is the loud music Overreach
Strict rein azure Marall Sir
What what youl say unhappy
Cauld cauld wind blaw hail
Old Ballad Billy what then
Lean to life auld sit by fire

Boiled milk was greatly
appreciated a step on the
road to luxury and there
was slim made of bitter
potatoes broken up when
kindly cottagers strove
to cherish and welcome
Patrick Brontë's childhood
Their guest strove well

Homemade bread was
fadge the raised soda
bap or scone came later
baked on a griddle or
girdle while baking was
called "harning" but
mashing up potatoes
in meal and flour was
called "baking"

Advanced from Emdale cabin

to Lisnacreevy cottage neither

sought nor accepted sympathy

Hoarded his savings he didn't

dread hobgoblins Mrs. Gaskell

exaggerated the facts in this

matter as have many others

Carried his webs to Banbridge

Could weave and read at once

At supper sowans fine enough to
thread a needle the Brontë mind
never ran smoothly his children
were given ghost stories monsters
I am grateful archaeology Galway
oral history warcry boat curragh
When stealthy in shawl slumber
speaking from memory set forth
by moonlight written fact Irish
only in name limestone traveller

Book I am sorry fair

Covering have fallen

Silent O Moyle fair

maiden by cloudlight

Book I am sorry yet

say we recollect it

in *Tenant*

aary the escaped of you

Irish oral history here

stealthy shawl slumber

kin to small scarp fact

Fisherman seaweed seven

forth the name Novembe

Reader of poetry this book
contains all poetry THOOR
BALLYLEE seven notes for
stage representation May
countryside you reader of
poetry that I am forgotten
Long notes seem necessary
Unworthy players ask for
legend familiar in legend
the arrow king and no king

A character walks on thatch

bridge across the deep stage

Material image and her mate

Chanting within her role she

cannot step beyond invisible

right foot lifted in half step

Where is he going because this

play is famous for April sage

green kagota kneeling piety is

a dominant restraint he does

not stoop as in pitiful reign

Noh lies in its concentration

You child of Atsumori old cloak

faded gown sleeve flung open

Fabled founder in darkness
in Greek authentic helmet
Illumination his heirs and
assigns forever as if wives
in themselves loosened the
murderous shawl so they act
astonishment but all terror
exactly as I have written I
am in ash blue gray Kogota
costume and the one here who
is the child Chorus comes in
Now Ireland in rebellion I
am arrived at upper memory
eroded base on shallow step

The child of Atsumori old coat

faded gown sleeve flung open

Maternal image and her mate

Where is he going because the

play is famous for April sage

green kagota under two cross

sticks the apparition a young

girl's ghost the boy's mother

Double play of double meaning

Noh lies in its concentration

Change and all chance perilous

Winnowing each slip for re-
appearance father and child
Fling sleeve together sit down
Actor-author setting out no
turn away obedient as Chorus
listening to Chorus familiar
step movement of feet pivot-
change costume lyric portion
a subtle voice effect a voice
Tattered coat our journey out

All that is and all that is
Listen listen map all that
sea are you looking at sea
Goading ice wind arrowly
am I to fear the waves or
is memory cradle cradle

Whippoorwill you song so
native to my own freely

I am still moving one wave
twicewashed these are pas-
times voice of evening half
local gold half peregrine red
Where the escaped and their
frolic nobody knows aslant
Style in one stray sitting I
approach sometime in plain
handmade rag wove costume
awry what I long for array

Illustrations

p. ix   Interleaf and title page of John Manning's copy of Robert Louis Stevenson, *The Master of Ballantrae* (London: Cassell and Company, Ltd., 1894).

p. x   Mirror image of previous illustration.

p. 1   Mrs. Bury Palliser, *History of Lace* (New York: Charles Scribner's Sons, 1902), fig. 52: Isabella Clara Eugenia, Daughter of Phillip II, Archduchess of Austria, Governess of the Netherlands, died 1633.

p. 2   *History of Lace,* fig. 99: detail of lace (Ave Maria, Dieppe).

p. 41   Illustrations from Mary Manning's copies of George MacDonald, *At the Back of the North Wind* (London: Blackie and Son Ltd.) *(left)* and Robert Louis Stevenson, *A Child's Garden of Verses,* illus. by Charles Robinson (New York: Charles Scribner's Sons, 1909) *(right).*

p. 42   Charles Sanders Peirce, ms 495., 1898.

p. 47   Page from Nathan Bailey's *An Universal Etymological English Dictionary* (London: R. Ware, 1753).

p. 48   Frontispiece and interleaf, Rev. John Todd, *The Lost Sister of Wyoming, An Authentic Narrative* (Northampton: J. H. Butler, 1842; anonymous illustration with caption: "The Lost Sister still lives in her wild home on the Missisineway River").

p. 50   Mary Manning, circa 1924, from Irish family photograph album.

p. 53   Interleaf and photograph of John Singer Sargent's portrait of Ellen Terry as Lady Macbeth, in Mary Manning's copy of Bram Stoker, *Personal Reminiscences of Henry Irving,* Vol. II (New York and London: The Macmillan Company, 1906).

p. 55   John Manning, circa 1940, from Irish family photograph album.

176

p. 85   Bennett house, "Undercliff," in Killiney, from Irish family photo album *(left)*; anonymous frontispiece from *The Lost Sister* (as on pp. 42, 62, 68) *(right)*.

p. 86   Material pasted at front of John Manning's *Alice.*

p. 87   Mary Ferrar, 1617, from the portrait by Cornelius Janssen at Magdalene College, Cambridge, in *Nicholas Ferrar of Little Gidding,* A. L. Maycock (London: Society for Promoting Christian Knowledge, 1938).

p. 111   "Unfinished Drawn-work" from *History of Lace,* fig. 34.

p. 113   Pages from the same books as on p. 41.

p. 117   Portrait of unknown man formerly known as Michael Drayton, by unknown artist.

p. 119   Photograph of Mary Manning, circa 1913. Caption reads: "Watching an aeroplane/Mary Manning."

p. 119   The first page of Mary Manning's last address book.

p. 126   Emily Dickinson fragment ms. 169.

p. 128   The cover of John Manning's *The Dramatic Works of Richard Sheridan,* Henry Frowde (Oxford: Oxford University Press, 1906), and interleaf/photo of Henry Irving as Charles I from Stoker's *Personal Reminiscences.*

p. 130   Frontispiece portrait of Nicholas Ferrar, engraved by C. J. Tomkins, after the picture by Janssen at Magdalene College, Cambridge, with interleaf, in *The Story Books of Little Gidding Being The Religious Dialogues Recited in the Great Room, 1631–2, From the Original Manuscript of Nicholas Ferrar* (New York: E.P. Dutton and Co., 1899).

p. 131   Pages from John Manning's *Alice.*

p. 132   Fanny and Susan Howe, Annisquam, Massachusetts, circa 1944.

p. 136   The Bennett family.

p. 137   Flyleaf and illustration of Robert Louis Stevenson's *The Strange Case of Dr. Jekyll and Mr. Hyde* (New York: Charles Scribner's Sons, 1886).

p. 140   Mary Manning's bookmark on last two poems of Yeats, *Later Poems.*

p. 141   Photograph of ruins at the corner of Sackville Street and Eden Quay, with monument of Daniel O'Connell, from *The Rebellion in Dublin,*

177

April, 1916, a pamphlet published at the time by Eason & Son, Ltd., Dublin and Belfast. Background is the cover of the book *Percy French: Prose, Poems, and Parodies,* edited by his sister Mrs. De Burgh Daly (Dublin: The Talbot Press, 1929).

p. 143   John Manning's illustration to pages 158–59 of *Alice.*

p. 144   *Ballantrae* frontispiece and interleaf.

p. 147   Mary Manning, circa 1913.